W9-AVK-310

FOR
LOU,
THE BEST LAND
DESIGNER!

urbanism in the age of climate change

by peter calthorpe

peter calthorpe

urbanism
in the age of
climate change

ISLANDPRESS

Washington | Covelo | London

ISLAND PRESS is a trademark of the Center for Resource Economics.

Library of Congress Cataloging-in-Publication Data

Calthorpe, Peter.
    Urbanism in the age of climate change / Peter Calthorpe.
        p. cm.
    Includes bibliographical references and index.
    ISBN-13: 978-1-59726-720-5 (cloth : alk. paper)
    ISBN-10: 1-59726-720-1 (cloth : alk. paper)
    ISBN-13: 978-1-59726-721-2 (pbk. : alk. paper)
    ISBN-10: 1-59726-721-X (pbk. : alk. paper)
    1. Urban ecology (Sociology)—United States. 2. Community development, Urban—Environmental aspects—United States. 3. City planning—Environmental aspects—United States. 4. Sustainable development—United States. I. Title.
HT167.C32 2010
307.1'4160973--dc22   2010021982

Printed using Old Style 7
Book design and graphics by L Studio
Infographics support by Gavin Potenza

Printed on recycled, acid-free paper ♲

Manufactured in the United States of America
10 9 8 7 6 5 4 3 2 1

Keywords: Buckminster Fuller, carbon emissions, ecological footprint, environmental conservation, green urbanism, housing affordability, mixed-use development, New Urbanism, regional planning, renewable energy, smart growth, sustainable transportation, urban footprint, Vision California, walkable communities, whole-systems design

For Asa, Lucia, and Jacob, who will inherit the challenge.

contents

acknowledgments

This book represents a forty year odyssey that has involved many teachers, collaborators, and friends. The list is long but a few individuals were critical to the evolution of this field and my personal progress. Foremost was Sim Van der Ryn, truly the father of sustainable communities. Sim's pioneering leadership in the 1970s launched and defined the field, and gave me my first opportunity to practice urban design.

It takes a community to advance work of this nature … it is never a solo act. And for me the Congress for the New Urbanism (CNU) has provided a community, a sounding board, many challenges, endless support, and a long list of dear friends. As the CNU has grown over the last twenty years, my group of friends and colleagues there has remained steadfast and deeply important to me.

Closer to home, the staff and partners at Calthorpe Associates have provided the substance of so much of this work. My partner Joe Scanga has been working for twenty years to realize this vision and has been the driver of much of our success. The brilliant work of Joe DiStefano, in planning and development of new analytical tools, has been critical to our efforts. Danny Yadegar provided extraordinary support as a research assistant and Erika Lew provided analysis, in-depth reviews, and invaluable brainstorming.

Many old friends provided unique and essential help on this book. Marianna Leuschel not only created the bold graphic design for the book but also provided the vision to translate so much complex data into a legible form and invaluable feedback on content. Stewart Brand, a though leader and personal mentor for years, contributed insightful feedback and encouragement. Doug Kelbaugh, a friend from the days of passive solar design, spent weeks editing, commenting on, and pushing my early drafts toward a clarity I am sure I would have never attained without him. Jonathon Rose, a close part of my family, supported me with his parallel efforts and insightful dialogue. Tom Adams of the California League of Conservation Voters reviewed my drafts but more importantly was a key instigator of SB375 California's landmark bill to link land-use and carbon emissions, and therefore the underlying analysis presented here.

Heather Boyer at Island Press not only brought order to what began as rambling thoughts but also was the first motivator and advocate for the book. Without her this would not have happened.

Ultimately my family has provided the foundation and essential support for this effort. They tolerated the wandering mind, and the endless absences at odd times that work like this involves for one like me. My wife Jean Driscoll provided an extraordinary balance of love, centering, and critical thought. She kept me sane and happy. My children Asa, Lucia, and Jacob give me the most profound sense of purpose and the ultimate reward, love and hope.

In this book, I define the term urbanism broadly—by qualities, not quantities; by diversity, not size; by intensity, not density; by connectivity, not just location.

I am still motivated by something Bucky Fuller, America's iconoclastic engineer and inventor, advocated in the 1950s and 1960s. It was not his geodesic domes, dymaxion houses, or crazy three-wheeled cars, but an idea more fundamental to his thinking: whole systems design. Long before we saw a satellite view of earth, Bucky was talking about "spaceship earth"—an engineer's metaphor for the ultimate ecological paradigm. His metaphor was complex and implied many things: that we are all in this together, that our planet is indivisible and interdependent, and that we are in charge, responsible, at the helm. We are not at the mercy of Mother Earth but occupy a place somewhere between steward and pilot. As climate change now presses down on us, this metaphor becomes even more compelling, challenging, and important.

During Bucky's time, we were having a romance with engineering; efficiency, mass production, standardization, and specialization were the themes of the age. It was a mechanical, cause-and-effect worldview—no complex feedback loops, no uncertainty, no ecology. In fact, half the globe—the communists—thought they could engineer the world's social structure and economy as well as its industries. Our half believed in, as Adam Smith called it, a more mysterious "invisible hand"—perhaps a nod to a religious worldview or the humility that we could not control everything. Nevertheless, after World War II, both sides let the engineers run things, optimizing production, mass-producing everything from houses and toasters to tomatoes, and letting specialists construct vast labyrinths out of their institutional silos.

But Bucky was a different kind of engineer. He wanted to "do more with less," to pierce through the silos. He infected us all with the notion that all things are connected, that there is no such thing as waste, and that the more comprehensive we make systems the more sustainable they are. Perhaps most important for me was his optimism—that we could design ecological solutions, that technology could be on our side, that we could think in grand terms, and that we could make "spaceship earth" work for everyone. Some of these ideas are now common clichés, and that is a good thing. Toward the end of his life, Bucky started something called the World Game. This was an effort to engage a large number of professionals and policy makers in the challenge of devising sustainable global systems for food, water, and energy. In effect, that challenge is what we are facing now with climate change.

Superficially following his lead, I built a lot of leaky domes in the 1960s—and in so doing learned the difference between symbols and reality. In the next decade, I moved on to designing passive solar buildings (really doing more with less) and what Sim Van der Ryn called sustainable communities (a first pass at whole systems design at the neighborhood level). These approaches matured into Transit-Oriented Development (TOD) and New Urbanism in the 1990s, and finally to the notion of regional cities. Each step built on the previous thinking and expanded its range and impact.

In terms of the energy and climate change challenge we now face, each step revealed opportunities that could not be met at the previous scale. Efficient, climate-responsive buildings are important but miss many community-scale opportunities. Individual communities, while offering more options for whole systems design, cannot in themselves create robust alternatives to the car nor enact large-scale strategies for farmland preservation, habitat conservation, or economic revitalization. TODs began to imply a regional framework of transit and intelligently located development but were ultimately just one dimension of a broad range of strategies needed to shape healthy regional growth. Over decades, I learned that each scale depends on the others and that only a whole systems approach, with each scale nesting into the other, can deliver the kind of transformation we now need to confront climate change. This book is, I hope, a summary and synthesis of all these lessons, a set of tools to craft a different future and the metric of just what is at stake.

Like it or not, the globe has an urban future. The world's urban population has more than quadrupled since 1950, more than half live in urban environments for the first time, and the trend is accelerating.[1] The pressing question, then, is what type of urbanism will prevail. The answer not only will define the physical nature of our communities but will prescribe our environmental footprint as well as frame our social opportunities and underwrite our economic future. Yet, urbanism is often missing from the proposed remedies for climate change, job growth, and environmental stress; it is the invisible wedge in the pie chart of green solutions.

In this book, I define the term *urbanism* broadly—by qualities, not quantities; by intensity, not density; by connectivity, not just location. Urbanism is always made from places that are mixed in uses, walkable, human scaled, and diverse in population; that balance cars with transit; that reinforce local history; that are adaptable; and that support a rich public life. Urbanism can come in many forms, scales, locations, and densities. Many of our traditional villages, streetcar suburbs, country towns, and historic cities are "urban" by this definition. Urbanism often resides beyond our downtowns.

While urbanism will vary by geography, culture, and economy, traditional urbanism always manifests the vitality, complexity, and intimacy that defined our finest cities and towns for centuries. By this definition suburbs can be "urban" if they are walkable and mixed use, and cities can easily be the reverse—just visit any central paradigm. Finally, this book reports on efforts in California to limit greenhouse gas emissions systemically through land use policy, industrial standards, and technological innovation—a project called Vision California.

The great recession of 2008, and its underlying real estate meltdown, was more than just a crisis of credit structures and banking policies. It was a manifestation of a deeper reality: that many of our communities and lifestyles are unsustainable—too auto dependent, too land intensive, too isolated, and, in the end, too expensive to own and operate. Our development patterns became as toxic as the financial structures that underwrote them. In plain fact, our land use patterns were, and still remain, precariously out of sync with our most profound economic, social, and environmental needs.

Responding to climate change and our coming energy challenge without a more sustainable form of urbanism will be impossible.

Urbanism and Climate Change
Chapter 1

I take as a given that climate change is an imminent threat and
potentially catastrophic—the science is now clear that we are day by day contributing to our own demise. In addition, I believe that an increase in fuel costs due to declining oil reserves is also inevitable. The combination of these two global threats presents an economic and environmental challenge of unparalleled proportions—and, lacking a response, the potential for dire consequences. These challenges will in turn bring into urgent focus the way our buildings, towns, cities, and regions shape our lives and our environmental footprint. Beyond a transition to clean energy sources, I believe that urbanism—compact, diverse, and walkable communities—will play a central role in addressing these twin threats. In fact, responding to climate change and our coming energy challenge without a more sustainable form of urbanism will be impossible.

Many deny either the timing or the reality of these challenges. They argue that global demand for oil will not outstrip production and that climate change is overstated, nonexistent, or somehow not related to our actions. Setting aside such debates, this book accepts the premise that both climate change and peak oil are pressing realities that need aggressive solutions.

The two challenges are deeply linked. The science tells us that if we are to arrest climate change, our goal for carbon emissions should be just 20 percent of our 1990 level by 2050. That, combined with a projected U.S. population increase of 130 million people,[1] means each person in 2050 would need to be emitting on average just 12 percent of his or her current greenhouse gases (GHG)—what I will call here the "12% Solution."[2] If we can achieve the 12% Solution to offset climate change, we will simultaneously reduce our fossil-fuel dependence and demonstrate a sustainable model of prosperity. Such a low-carbon future will inherently reduce oil demands at rates that will allow a smoother transition to alternative fuels—and the next economy.

In addition to these twin environmental challenges, the United States has two other systemic forces to reckon with in the next generation: an aging population and a more diverse middle class with less wealth. We are now a country in which a third of the population are baby boomers or older and less than a quarter are traditional families with kids. And for the past decade, median income has actually fallen; in fact, "the typical American household saw its inflation-adjusted income decline by more than $2,000 between 1999 and 2008."[3] So, at the same time that we must respond to climate change and rising energy costs, we must also adjust our housing stock to fit a changing demographic and find a more frugal form of prosperity.

Such a transformation will require deep change, not just in energy sources, technology, and conservation measures but also in urban design, culture, and lifestyles. More than just deploying green technologies and adjusting our thermostats, it will involve rethinking the way we live and the underlying form of our communities. The good news is that our environmental, social, and economic challenges have a shared solution in urbanism. Shaping regions that reduce oil dependence simultaneously reduces carbon emissions, costs less for the average household, and creates healthy, integrated places for our seniors: one solution for multiple challenges.

The urban solution involves both technology and design. For example, we will need to dramatically reduce the number of miles we drive as well as develop less carbon intensive vehicles. It will mean living and working in buildings that demand significantly less energy as well as powering them with renewable sources. It will involve the kinds of food we eat, the kinds of homes we build, the ways we travel, and the kinds of communities we inhabit. It will certainly involve giving up the idea of any single "silver bullet" solution (whether solar or nuclear, conservation or carbon capture, adaptation or mitigation) and understanding that such a transformation will involve all of the above—and, perhaps most important, that they are all interdependent.

In fact, the viability of new technologies and clean energy sources will depend on the success of our conservation efforts at the regional, community, and building scales, which in turn will be determined by our basic lifestyles and the urban forms that support our changing demographics. The key will be designing the right mix of strategies, a "whole systems" rather than a "checklist" approach to climate change, energy, and economics.

There are three interdependent approaches to these nested challenges: lifestyle, conservation, and clean energy. Lifestyle involves how we live—the way we get around, the size of our homes, the foods we eat, and the quantity of goods we consume. These depend in turn on the type of communities we build and the culture we inhabit—degrees of urbanism. Conservation revolves around technical efficiencies—in our buildings, cars, appliances, utilities, and industrial systems—as well as preserving the natural resources that support us all, our global forests, ocean ecologies, and farmlands. These conservation measures are simple, they save money, and they are possible now. The third fix, clean energy, is what we have been most focused on: new technologies for solar, wind, wave, geothermal, biomass, and even a new generation of nuclear power or fusion. These energy sources are sexy, they are relatively expensive, and they will be available sometime soon. All three approaches will be essential, but here I focus on the first two—lifestyle and conservation—because they are, in the end, our most cost effective and easily available tools.

The intersection of lifestyle and conservation is urbanism. Consider that in the United States industry represents 29 percent of our GHG emissions; agriculture and other non-energy-related activities, just 9 percent; and freight and planes, another 9 percent. This 47 percent total represents the GHG emissions of the products we buy, the food we eat, the embodied energy of all our possessions, and all the shipping involved in getting them to us. The remaining 53 percent depends on the nature of our buildings and personal transportation system—the realm of urbanism.[4] As a result, urbanism, along with a simple combination of transit and more efficient buildings and cars, can deliver much of our needed GHG reductions.

Perhaps just as important as greenhouse gas reductions and oil savings is the fact that urbanism generates a fortuitous web of co-benefits—it is our most potent weapon against climate change because it does so much more. Urbanism's compact forms lead to less land consumed and more farmland, parks, habitat, and open space preserved. A smaller urban footprint results in less development costs and fewer miles of roads, utilities, and services to build and maintain, which then leads to fewer impervious surfaces, less polluted storm runoff, and more water directed back into aquifers.

More compact development leads to lower housing costs as lower land and infrastructure costs affect sales prices and taxes. Urban development means a different mix of housing types—fewer large single-family lots; more bungalows and townhomes—but in the end provides more housing choices for a more diverse population. It means less private space but more shared community places—more efficient and less expensive overall. Urbanism is more suited to an aging population, for whom driving and yard maintenance are a growing burden, and for working families seeking lower utility bills and less time spent commuting.

Urbanism leads to fewer miles driven, which then leads to less gas consumed and less dependence on foreign oil supplies, less air pollution, less carbon emissions. Fewer miles also leads to less congestion, lower emissions, lower road construction and maintenance costs, and fewer auto accidents. This then leads to lower health costs because of fewer accidents and cleaner air, which is reinforced by more walking, bicycling, and exercising, which in turn contributes to lower obesity rates. And more walking leads to more people on the streets, safer neighborhoods, and perhaps stronger communities.

The feedback loops go on. More urban development means more compact buildings—less energy needed to heat and cool, lower utility bills, less irrigation water, and, once again, less carbon in the atmosphere. This then leads to lower demands on electric utilities and fewer new power plants, which again results in less carbon and fewer costs. As Bucky Fuller exhorted us, urbanism is inherently "doing more with less." Or, as Mies van der Rohe famously asserted, "Less is more."

But for the past fifty years, our economy and society have been operating on the premise that "more is more" and "bigger is better": bigger homes, bigger yards, bigger cars with bigger engines, bigger budgets, bigger institutions, and, finally, bigger energy sources. In contrast, urbanism naturally tends toward a "small is beautiful" philosophy. This then involves trade-offs: less private space but perhaps a richer public realm; less private security but perhaps a safer community; less auto mobility but more convenient transit. Compact development does mean smaller yards, fewer cars, and less private space for some. On the other hand, it can dramatically reduce everyday costs and leave more time for family and community. The question is not which is right and which is wrong or that it must be all one way or the other—urbanism works best with blends. The question is how such trade-offs fit with our emerging demographics, our desires, our needs, our economic means—and perhaps our sense of what a good life really is.

Vision California

Measuring and understanding the feedback loops and co-benefits of urbanism are critical to judging these trade-offs. Few comprehensive studies have brought all of these variables together, so we typically cannot understand the relationships and see all the implications. Fortunately, California's effort to implement its new greenhouse gas reduction laws has provided a comprehensive look at urbanism and its potential in relation to a range of conservation and clean energy policies. The Vision California study, developed for the California High Speed Rail Authority and the California Strategic Growth Council, measured the results of several statewide land use futures coupled with conservation policies through the year 2050.[5] The results make concrete the choices before us, the feedback loops, and the scale of both benefits and costs.

California is projected to grow by 7 million new households and 20 million people, to a population of nearly 60 million, by 2050.[6] It is currently the eighth-largest economy in the world and therefore provides an important model of what is possible. The study compared a "Trend" future dominated by the state's now typical low-density suburban growth and conservative conservation policies to a "Green Urban" alternative. This Green Urban alternative assumed that 35 percent of growth would be urban infill; 55 percent would be formed from a more compact, mixed-use, and walkable form of suburban expansion; and only 10 percent would be standard low-density development. In addition, the Green Urban alternative would push the auto fleet to an average 55 miles per gallon (MPG), its fuel would contain one third less carbon, and all new buildings would be 80 percent more efficient than today's norm. It does not represent a green utopia, but it is heading in that direction. The results of this comparison highlight just how much is at stake and what the costs will be.

Remarkably, the quantity of land needed to accommodate the next two generations was reduced 67 percent by the Green Urban scenario, from more than 5,600 square miles in the Trend future to only 1,850 square miles. By comparison, the state's current developed area is 5,300 square miles.[7] This difference would save vast areas (up to 900 square miles) of farmland in the Central Valley along with key open space and habitat in the coastal regions of the state. The more compact future means smaller yards to irrigate and fewer parking lots to landscape, saving an average of 3.4 million acre-feet of water per year—enough to fill the San Francisco Bay annually or to irrigate 5 million acres of farmland.[8] Less developed land also translates to fewer miles of infrastructure to build and maintain. The annual savings would be around $194 billion for the state, or $24,300 for each new household—not including the costs of ongoing maintenance. In addition, the Trend future would cost more in police and fire services as coverage areas increase.

Surprisingly, such a future would not dramatically change the range of housing choices available in the state. In fact, some would argue that the outcome would be more market responsive, providing a long overdue adjustment of housing types and prices. Specifically, while large single-family lots would decline from 40 percent of the total today to 30 percent in 2050, small-lot homes and bungalows would increase slightly and townhomes would double to 15 percent. Multifamily flats, condos, and apartments would actually end up the same, at around a third of the market. Overall, detached single-family homes would drop from 62 percent of all homes today to just over half. Many would conclude that this would be a reasonable shift, one ultimately making the housing stock more diverse and affordable—not, as some would argue, the end of the American dream.

In the Green Urban future, auto dependence drops dramatically—in fact, average vehicle miles traveled throughout the state would be reduced 34 percent, to 18,000 miles per household, from a Trend projection of 27,200. Closer destinations, better transit service, and more walkable neighborhoods all contribute to this significant shift. We would all still have cars, but they would be more efficient and we would use them less. The implication of this reduction in auto use is far-reaching. In terms of congestion, it is the equivalent of taking over 15 million cars off the road.[9] There would be fewer roads and parking lots built, less land covered with impervious surface, and less runoff water to be cleaned and stored. The list of collateral benefits is long. In fact, the need for new freeways, highways, and arterials is reduced by 23,000 lane-miles, a saving of around $450 billion for the state.

Less driving means fewer accidents, in this scenario potentially saving around 3,100 lives and $5 billion in associated costs per year.[10] Less driving means less air pollution and less respiratory disease.[11] More walking means healthier bodies and less obesity, affecting diabetes rates and all of its associated health costs.[12]

Most significantly, the Green Urban scenario reduces carbon emissions and comes very close to achieving the 12% Solution in the transportation sector of the economy. When the savings in vehicle miles traveled are combined with low-carbon/high-MPG cars, emissions for transportation drop from more than 260 million metric tons (MMT) to just 29. Moreover, we would consume 352 billion fewer gallons of fuel over the next forty years, for a saving of over $2.1 trillion. These numbers are almost too big to imagine, but by way of comparison, the proposed high-speed rail system running from San Diego to San Francisco is projected to cost $42 billion, less than one-fifth the value of the potential annual gas savings. Put simply, at a projected $8 per gallon in 2050, these gas savings represent around $6,100 in savings per household.

There is more. The efficient and compact buildings of urban development use less energy, produce fewer greenhouse gases, and cost less to operate. The carbon reduction in the building sector is projected to be over 62 percent less, not enough to achieve its share of the 12% Solution but a significant and necessary step. In total, the average household in the Green Urban future would save around $1,000 a year in utility payments. When this figure is combined with reduced auto ownership, maintenance, insurance, and gas costs, California households would save close to $11,000 a year in current dollars. With an interest rate of 5 percent in 2050, this could pay a mortgage of $200,000.

What is not to like in such a Green Urban future? For some, exactly the thing that makes most of these savings possible: a more urban life.

Urbanism Expanded

For many people, *urban* is a bad word that implies crime, congestion, poverty, and crowding. For them, it represents an environment that moves people away from a healthy connection with nature and the land. Its stereotype is the American ghetto, a crime-ridden concrete jungle that simultaneously destroys land, community, and human potential. The reaction to this stereotype has been a middle-class retreat into the closeted world of single-family lots and gated subdivisions in the suburbs. As a result, much of the last half century's planning has been directed toward depopulating cities, whether through the satellite towns of Europe or the suburbs of America.

But, for many others, the word *urban* represents economic opportunity, culture, vitality, innovation, and community. This positive reading is now manifest in the revitalized centers of many of our historic cities. In these core areas, the public domain—with its parks, walkable streets, commercial centers, arts, and institutions—is once again becoming rich and vibrant, valued and desirable. There is new life in many city centers and their public places, from cafés and plazas to urban parks and museums—ultimately drawing people back to the city.

In fact, since 2000, many of our major cities have increased their share of new home construction while their region's suburbs have declined. For example, in 2008, Portland issued 38 percent of all the building permits within its region, compared to an average of 9 percent in the early 1990s; Denver accounted for 32 percent, up from 5 percent; and Sacramento accounted for 27 percent, up from 9 percent. There is an even stronger trend toward urban redevelopment in the largest metropolitan regions. New York City accounted for 63 percent of the building permits issued within its region. By comparison, the city averaged about 15 percent of regional building permits during the early 1990s. Similarly, Chicago now accounts for 45 percent of the building permits within its region, up from just 7 percent in the early 1990s.[13] This represents a dramatic turnaround as cities regain their roles as centers of innovation, social mobility, artistic creativity, and economic opportunity.

Urbanism of this caliber is desirable but, unfortunately, too often limited and very expensive. A home in the metropolitan center is, in some places, the most valuable in the region—an economic signal of just how desirable good urban places can be. In such cities as New York, Portland, Seattle, or Washington, DC, urban residences command a premium of 40 to 200 percent per square foot over their suburban alternative.[14] Meanwhile, in our ghettos and first-ring suburbs, the working poor—and now even the middle class—are suffering and struggling. Urbanism is again proving its value; but if in limited supply, it soon can become too valuable.

At the same time, the bread-and-butter subdivisions at the metropolitan fringe experienced the greatest fall in value during the 2008 housing bust.[15] Their physical environments along with their economic opportunities, cost of transportation, and social structures are becoming more and more stressed. Many economic and social factors are at work in this equation, but certainly a better form of urbanism is one necessary component of the renewal we need. But first, a clear definition of urbanism is needed.

Much confusion surrounds the differences between suburbs, sprawl, and what I mean by urbanism. Suburbs are not always sprawl and can be urban in many ways. Sprawl is a specific land use pattern of single-use zones, typically made up of subdivisions, office parks, and shopping centers strung together by arterials and highways. It is a landscape based on the automobile. We all know it when we see it; nevertheless, much of the debate about sprawl and urbanism is rife with misrepresentations.

For example, sprawl is typically described as discontinuous developments that wastefully hopscotches across the landscape. But healthy forms of suburban growth can also be discontinuous, as villages and towns with greenbelt separations demonstrate. Suburbs are criticized for their low densities, as if we should abolish single-family homes and yards, but many great urban places integrate a full range of densities, from large-lot mansions and single-family homes to bungalows and townhomes. The classic streetcar suburbs of the turn of the twentieth century were not sprawl—they were walkable, diverse in use, transit oriented, and compact—but they were relatively low density and outside the city center, in a word "suburban." Conversely, urban renewal programs transformed decaying urban districts into denser versions of suburban sprawl, substituting superblocks and arterials for walkable streets and single-income projects for complex, mixed-use neighborhoods.

It is the quality of the place that is most significant in sprawl: its relentless parking lots and oversized roads, uniform tracks of houses, isolated office parks, strip commercial areas, and, above all, its near total dependence on the car. To be against sprawl is not to be against suburbs or small towns. All suburbs are not sprawl, and unfortunately, not all sprawl is suburban.

Traditional urbanism has three essential qualities: (1) a diverse population and range of activities, (2) a rich array of public spaces and institutions, and (3) human scale in its buildings, streets, and neighborhoods. Most of our built environment, from city to suburb, manifested these traits prior to World War II. Now, most suburbs succeed in contradicting each trait; public space is withering for lack of investment, people and activities are segregated by simplistic zoning, and human scale is sacrificed to a ubiquitous accommodation of the car.

None of these urban design principles are new. Jane Jacobs postulated a similar definition of urbanism in her landmark 1961 work *The Death and Life of Great American Cities*. The difference here is that urban issues are also being considered in the context of climate change and environmental protection. In fact, one can arrive at the same design conclusions from the criteria of conservation, environmental quality, and energy efficiency that Jacobs located largely by social and cultural needs. By investigating the technologies and formal systems scaled for limited resources, climate change concerns add a new and critical element to Jacobs' rationale. If traditional urbanism and sustainable development can truly reduce our dependence on foreign oil, limit pollution and greenhouse gases, and create socially robust places, they not only will become desirable but will be inevitable.

To Jacobs' three traditional urban values of civic space, human scale, and diversity, the current environmental imperative adds two more: conservation and regionalism. Although the traditional city was by necessity energy and resource efficient, it commonly showed a destructive disregard for nature and habitat that would be inappropriate today. Bays were filled, wetlands drained, streams and rivers diverted, and key habitat destroyed. A green form of urbanism should protect those critical environmental assets while reducing overall resource demands.

Indeed, the simple attributes of urbanism are typically a more cost efficient environmental strategy than many renewable technologies. For example, in many climates, a party wall is more cost effective than a solar collector in reducing a home's heating needs. Well-placed windows and high ceilings offer better lighting than efficient fluorescents in the office. A walk or a bike ride is certainly less expensive and less carbon intensive than a hybrid car even at 50 MPG. A convenient transit line is a better investment than a "smart" highway system. A small cogenerating electrical plant that reuses its waste heat locally could save more carbon per dollar invested than a distant wind farm. A combination of urbanism and green technology will be necessary, but the efficiency of urbanism should precede the costs of alternate technologies.

As Amory Lovins of the Rocky Mountain Institute famously advocates, a "nega-watt" of conservation is always more cost effective than a watt of new energy, renewable or not. Urban living in its many forms turns out to be the best type of conservation.

In addition, the idea of "conservation" in urban design applies to more than energy, carbon, and the environment; it also implies preserving and repairing culture and history as well as ecosystems and resources. Conserving historic buildings, institutions, neighborhoods, and cultures is as essential to a vital, living urbanism as is preserving its ecological foundations.

Regionalism sets city and community into the contemporary reality of our expanding metropolis. At this point in history, most of our key economic, social, and environmental networks extend well beyond individual neighborhoods, jurisdictions, or even cities. Our cultural identity, open space resources, transportation networks, social links, and economic opportunities all function at a regional scale—as do many of our most challenging problems, including crime, pollution, and congestion. Major public facilities, such as sports venues, universities, airports, and cultural institutions, shape the social geography of our regions as well as extend our local lives.

We all now lead regional lives, and our metropolitan form and governance need to reflect that new reality. In fact, urbanism can thrive only within the construct of a healthy regional structure. The tradition of urbanism must be extended to an interconnected and interdependent regional network of places, creating polycentric regions rather than a metropolis dominated by the old city/suburb schism.

This last point is critical to understanding urbanism and the climate change challenge. City life is not the only environmental option; a regional solution can offer a range of lifestyles and community types without compromising our ecology. A well-designed region, when combined with aggressive conservation strategies, extensive transit systems, and new green technologies, can offer many types of sustainable lifestyles. New York City may have among the smallest carbon footprint per capita, but to solve the climate change crisis we do not all have to live in the city.[16]

Identifying an appropriate balance among technology, urban design, and regional systems in confronting climate change is now the critical challenge. As a greater percentage of the world's population increases its wealth, the definition of prosperity will become critical. If progress translates into the old American suburban lifestyle, we are all in trouble. If China and India adopt our development patterns—auto-oriented, low-density lifestyles or even a high-rise, high-density version of the same—we will truly need breakthrough technologies to accommodate the demands. If they develop an enlightened and indigenous form of urbanism, we all will have the opportunity to address climate change in a less heroic and more cost effective way.

In fact, many developing countries are fast approaching a tipping point of urbanism. As auto ownership grows, the infrastructure to support it expands. Slowly at first, then in a landslide, the logic of surface parking lots, low-density development, freeways, and malls becomes irresistible. As cars make remote destinations viable, the historic logic of density and urbanism erodes and the economics of single-use, low-density suburbs grows. The built environment shifts to focus on auto mobility in ways that are hard to reverse—and with this shift urban culture dies. Traditional landscapes and neighborhoods are demolished at astonishing rates to make way for what is now seen as modern. Certainly, we cannot romanticize or literally replicate the complex historic urban fabric of, say, the Hutong in Beijing, but we can learn from it.

At the center of energy and carbon problems in the United States (and in many developing countries in the not-too-distant future) is transportation. It represents almost a third of current U.S. GHG emissions and is the fastest-growing segment.[17] As industry becomes more efficient and jobs continue to shift toward an information economy, transportation becomes a more dominant issue.

It seems obvious that the more we spread out, the more we must drive. But the numbers are still startling. From 1980 to 2005, average miles driven per person increased by 50 percent in the United States, a change that can be linked to the nearly 20 percent increase in land consumed per person over roughly the same period.[18] By comparison, Portland, Oregon, with its regional focus on transit and walkable neighborhoods, has seen a reduction in vehicle miles traveled per capita since the mid-1990s.[19] At the same time that it reduced auto dependence, the Portland region has preserved valuable farmlands and provided a widening range of housing options. Short of such regional efforts, even a doubling of auto efficiency will not keep up with the typical growth in sprawl-induced travel. We cannot solve the carbon emission problem without changing our travel behavior, and to do that an alternative to our auto-dominated communities is essential.

The good news is that truly great urban places also happen to be the most environmentally benign form of human settlement and are at the heart of a green future. Cities and urban places produce the smallest carbon footprint on a per capita basis.[20] New Yorkers, for example, emit just a third of the GHG of the average American.[21] In addition, it is generally accepted that population growth in developing countries drops as a rural population urbanizes. Urbanism therefore leads to fewer people consuming fewer resources and emitting less GHG at a global scale. Urbanism is a climate change antibiotic and our most affordable solution to foreign oil dependence. *Urbanism is, in fact, our single most potent weapon against climate change, rising energy costs, and environmental degradation.*

Yet our towns, cities, and regions cannot be shaped around a single issue like climate change or peak oil, no matter how critical they may be. Urban design is part art, social science, political theory, engineering, geography, and economics. I believe it is necessarily all of the above—urban design cannot and should not be reduced to any single metric. In the end, great urban places are qualitative; they are ultimately defined by the coherence of their public places, the diversity of their population, and the opportunity they create for our collective aspirations. We will never treasure our cities and towns just because they are low carbon, energy efficient, or even economically abundant; we will treasure them only when we come to love them as places—as vessels of our cultural identities, stages for our social interaction, and landscapes for our personal narratives. But that does not mean that they should not also play a critical role in the climate change challenge.

Urbanism and Green Technology

I was part of the passive solar architectural movement in the 1970s. Its core idea was to provide energy for buildings in the most direct, elegant way. We had disdain for complicated "active solar" systems, with their complex engineering, maintenance, and costs. The passive way was first to reduce the demands by building tight, well-insulated structures, flooded with natural light, and then to let the sun's radiation or the cool night air work with the buildings' form to provide thermal comfort. The same approach needs to be taken in relation to the climate change challenge: we need to find the simple, elegant solutions that are based on conservation before we introduce complex technology, even if it is green.

We need to focus, ironically, on ends, not means. For example, in passive solar buildings, focusing on the end goal (thermal comfort) rather than the means (heating air) changed the design approach dramatically. It turns out that human comfort has more to do with surrounding surface temperatures than with air temperature in a building, so massive walls that absorb and store the sun's gentle heat also provide a more comfortable environment without all the hot air. Or, if lighting is the goal, electricity and bulbs are just one potential means; a building that welcomes daylight is the simple, elegant solution—even better than a complex system of wind farms generating green electrons for efficient fixtures. Likewise, the goal of transportation is access, not movement or mobility per se; movement is a means, not the end. So, bringing destinations closer together is a simpler, more elegant solution than assembling a new fleet of electric cars and the acres of solar collectors needed to power them. Call it "passive urbanism."

Once demands are reduced by passive urbanism, the next step is to add technology. Green urbanism is what you get when you combine the best of traditional urbanism with renewable energy sources, advanced conservation techniques, new green technologies, and integrated services and utilities. All the inherent benefits of urbanism can be amplified by a new generation of ecological design, smart grids, climate-responsive buildings, low-carbon or electric cars, and next-generation transit systems.

These technologies function in differing ways at differing scales. There are three scales of such green technology: building, community, and utility. Building-scale technologies are ecumenical; they can be applied in any form of development, traditional urban or auto-oriented sprawl. Obviously, better building insulation, weatherization, and efficient appliances can be used in single-family subdivisions as well as in urban townhomes. So, too, can solar domestic hot water systems or photovoltaic cells. Efficient lightbulbs make sense in any location, as do efficient appliances. While bigger, less efficient buildings will cost more to green, such retrofits and new building standards are the starting point for any sustainable future—but not the final solution.

At the other end of the spectrum are the centralized utility-scale systems. Shifting to massive renewable sources in remote locations will carry the burden of building equally massive distribution facilities. Such a "smart grid," while essential to moving large quantities of power to our cities from distant natural resource areas (wind, sun, geothermal), has a high capital cost and reduces efficiency because of transmission line losses. These expenses are in addition to costs that are already consistently higher than those of conservation. Also, large-scale solar and wind operations can create big environmental footprints, as large tracts of virgin land are developed.

What are the real needs for large utility-scale renewable energy sources? It depends on the type of communities we plan and how we build them. If we add the travel demand of an average single-family home in the United States to the energy needed to heat, cool, and power the home, the total is just under 400 million Btu (British thermal units) per year (this includes the source energy typically left out of these calculations: the embodied energy of cars, the energy to produce the gasoline, and the wasted energy to produce the home's electricity). Assume for argument that weatherization and greening this home can reduce building energy consumption by 30 percent and that the family buys new cars with 50 percent better mileage. The result is a 32 percent overall energy reduction—not bad for "green sprawl." In contrast, a typical townhome located in a walkable neighborhood (not necessarily downtown but near transit) without any solar panels or hybrid cars consumes 38 percent less energy than such a suburban single-family home. Traditional urbanism, even without green technology, is better than green sprawl.

Now add more building conservation measures, green technology, and better transit systems to the townhouse, and you get close to the results we will need in 2050. If you move to a green townhome in a transit village, you will be consuming 58 percent less energy than on a large lot in the suburbs. If you move to a green condo in the city, you will be saving 73 percent when compared to the average single-family home in a distant suburb.

The implications of this for our power grid are massive. If more families lived this way—say just a quarter moved from single-family lots to green townhomes—the generating capacity required for buildings in the nation would be reduced by over 25,000 megawatts per year, eliminating the need for 50 new 500-megawatt plants.[22]

At $1.3 million per megawatt of installed capacity, that is more than $32 billion of avoided capital cost for new power plants per year.[23] The reduced fuel costs and environmental impacts are additional benefits.

The same is true for auto use. For example, satisfying California's need for more driving in a "Trend" future would result in around 183 billion additional auto miles per year in 2050 when compared to the more urban alternative. Some believe that if we shifted to electric cars running on green electrons, the carbon problem could be solved. However, producing that many green electrons has a hidden hurdle: it would take 50,000 acres of high-efficiency solar thermal plants, 130,000 acres of photovoltaic panels, or 860,000 acres of wind farms (nearly thirty times the land area of San Francisco) to power such a transportation system.[24] This would present a giant environmental footprint no matter where it was placed. Ironically, the biggest barrier to such a green, if not urban, solution may be environmentalists themselves, protesting lost desert landscapes or resisting impacts on bird populations by wind turbines (or even objecting to seeing the turbines on the horizon).

At the middle of the three scales, urbanism offers a better framework for more distributed community-scale energy systems. In fact, there are important community-scale systems that can function only within an urban framework. One of the most significant of these technologies is the decentralized cogeneration electric power plant (called combined heat and power, or CHP). Such small-scale power plants can be coupled with district heating and cooling systems to capture and use the generator's waste heat in local buildings and industry. Currently, for every watt of energy delivered to a home, two thirds is lost as waste heat up the smokestack and in transmission lines.[25] Local cogeneration plants coupled with district heating and cooling systems can largely eliminate these inefficiencies. The waste heat is captured and reused, while the transmission losses are greatly reduced. Because of this, it is estimated that cogeneration systems operate at around 90 percent efficiencies whereas standard power plants average only 40 percent.

Married to urban environments, cogeneration offers a cheap, time-tested alternative—one that has been employed by college campuses and European new towns for decades. There, small power plants are placed close to dense neighborhoods and commercial centers, distributing waste heat underground to each building for hot water, cooling, and heating. These plants can burn almost any form of renewable biomass, eliminating the energy-intensive process of converting valuable crops into biofuels or finding mechanisms to transform grass to gas. More interesting are a new generation of "waste to energy" technologies that not only produce green electricity and heat but also avoid the massive landfills and trucking costs of typical garbage systems.

Typically, cogeneration systems are found in commercial applications where waste heat is used in an industrial process and the power generation balances with the

Global Differences

In 2005 Americans emitted over 7 billion tons of greenhouse gas, or around 23 tons per person. The average American emits four times the global average and over twice that of comparable economies in Europe. And we account for over 30 percent of the carbon dumped into the atmosphere since 1850.

23   **10**   2   **4**

WORLD AVERAGE: **5.5** METRIC TONS

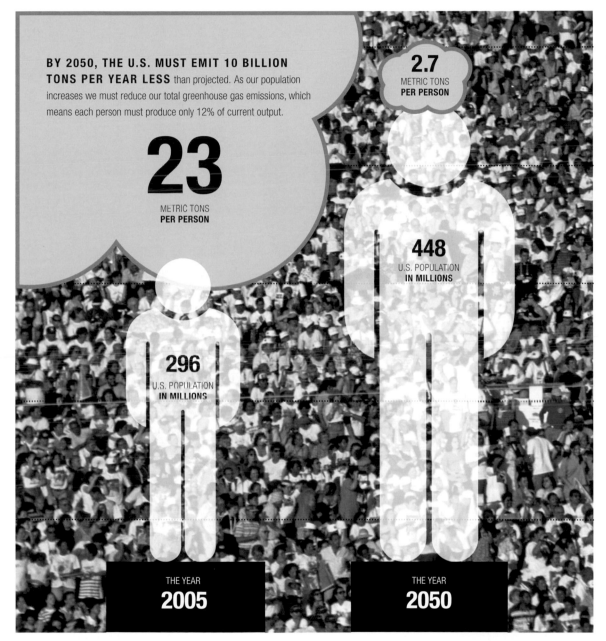

BY 2050, THE U.S. MUST EMIT 10 BILLION TONS PER YEAR LESS than projected. As our population increases we must reduce our total greenhouse gas emissions, which means each person must produce only 12% of current output.

23
METRIC TONS
PER PERSON

2.7
METRIC TONS
PER PERSON

448
U.S. POPULATION
IN MILLIONS

296
U.S. POPULATION
IN MILLIONS

THE YEAR
2005

THE YEAR
2050

The Challenge

If we are to arrest climate change at about 2° Celsius, developed countries must reduce carbon 80 percent from 1990 levels by 2050. Meanwhile, in the U.S. alone, population is projected to increase 140 million by 2050. That means that by 2050, per capita emissions must be reduced to just 2.7 metric tons per capita. To achieve this each person in 2050 must on average emit only 12 percent of their current rate.

the **12%** challenge

PLATE 1

the impact of
urbanism

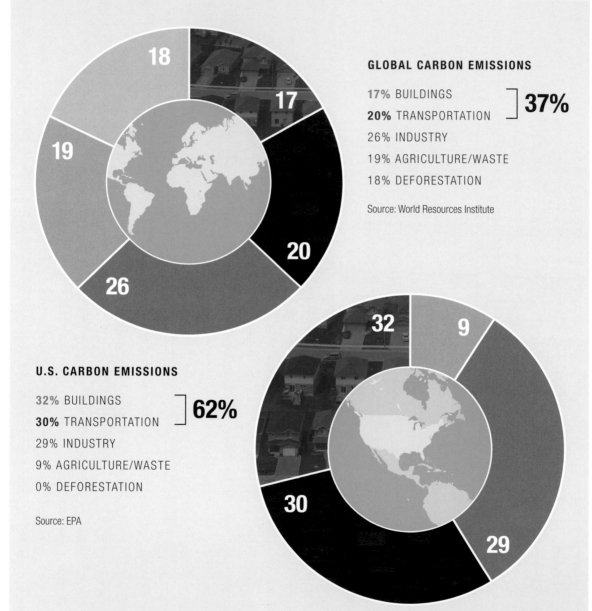

GLOBAL CARBON EMISSIONS

17% BUILDINGS ⎫
20% TRANSPORTATION ⎬ **37%**
26% INDUSTRY
19% AGRICULTURE/WASTE
18% DEFORESTATION

Source: World Resources Institute

U.S. CARBON EMISSIONS

32% BUILDINGS ⎫
30% TRANSPORTATION ⎬ **62%**
29% INDUSTRY
9% AGRICULTURE/WASTE
0% DEFORESTATION

Source: EPA

The non-energy-related emissions for the world from deforestation, agriculture, chemicals, and waste represent 37 percent of mankind's total impact. In the U.S. this segment is only 9 percent—hence our focus must be more on energy.

Globally, transportation represents 20 percent of GHG, but in the U.S. it is up to 30 percent and in California it almost doubles to 50 percent. The same is true of buildings; for the globe it is just 17 percent while in the U.S. it is 32 percent including its electric demands. The combination of buildings and transportation—urbanism—is two thirds of our challenge.

PLATE 2

- ■ buildings
- ■ transportation

Typical subdivision single-family home with three cars averaging 20 MPG driving 31,000 miles a year.
SUBURBAN

237   **162**

30 percent more energy-efficient single-family home with three cars averaging 30 MPG.
GREEN SUBURBAN

158   **113**

Townhome with two cars driving 15,500 Vehicle Miles Traveled (VMT)/year.
COMPACT

119   **126**

Energy-efficient townhome with two cars averaging 30 MPG
GREEN COMPACT

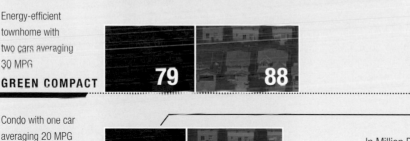

79   **88**

Condo with one car averaging 20 MPG driving 10,000 miles a year.
URBAN

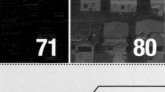

71   **80**

In Million British Thermal Units (MBTU)/year
Transportation carbon Includes oil refining as well as vehicle consumption.

Energy-efficient condo with one car averaging 30 MPG.
GREEN URBAN

47   **56**

In MBTU/year
The household building energy numbers account for source (or input) energy. All figures represent national averages.

The sum of energy consumed in an average home (heating, cooling, appliances, and auto) reveals radical differences. A large single-family home in the suburbs with three cars would use close to 400 MBTU per year. The same home with conservation features and efficient cars would bring it down to 270 MBTU. In contrast a townhome in a mixed-use neighborhood with convenient transit and only two cars would need 245 MBTU, less than the "green suburban" home. If that "urban" home used solar, conservation, and efficient autos it would be down to just 167 MBTU—a threefold savings. A green condo in the city would perform on average 75 percent better than the suburban home.

PLATE 3

comparing
neighborhoods

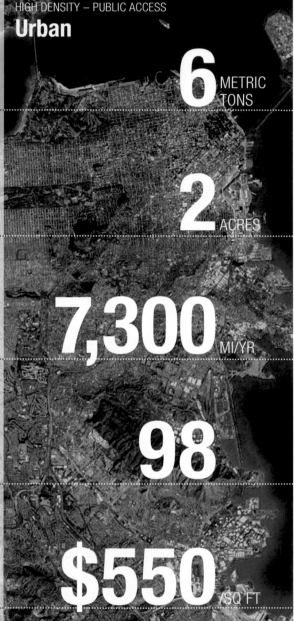

Urban

Average for a household's transportation and heating in Bay Area.
ANNUAL CARBON EMISSIONS

6 METRIC
TONS

The net area for 100
units of housing.
LAND CONSUMPTION

2 ACRES

Average per house based
on odometer readings.
HOUSEHOLD VMT

7,300 MI/YR

Measures walkable proximity of local
commercial destinations. 100 points
represents best access.
WALK SCORE

98

Average value per square foot
from recorded sales prices.
PROPERTY VALUE

$550 /SQ FT

Russian Hill, San Francisco This neighborhood in the heart
of the city averages only three stories but is dense by suburban
standards, has a great mix of shops, restaurants, and services,
and is a short transit ride from downtown.

PLATE 4

The varied urban lifestyles within any metropolitan region can result in vast environmental and economic differences. Where one lives determines the amount of land developed, the quantity of infrastructure that must be built, your average amount of auto use, the amount you can walk, and in many cases the cost of your housing. Here are three middle-class neighborhoods across the San Francisco Bay Area that reveal striking differences.

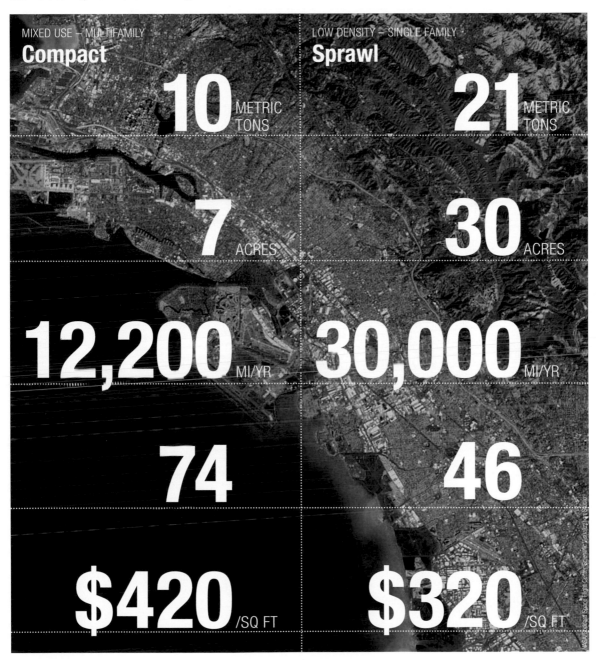

MIXED USE – MULTIFAMILY
Compact
10 METRIC TONS
7 ACRES
12,200 MI/YR
74
$420 /SQ FT

LOW DENSITY – SINGLE FAMILY
Sprawl
21 METRIC TONS
30 ACRES
30,000 MI/YR
46
$320 /SQ FT

Rockridge, Oakland This mixed-use area was created as a "street car suburb" back in the days of the historic key system. It is made up largely of bungalow, small-lot, single-family homes but has small apartment buildings at corners and a wonderful walkable main street along with a regional transit station at its center.

San Ramon, East Bay Area This community is a classic suburb with development patterns that fit the standard development paradigm: low-density single-family subdivisions, strip commercial arterials, single-story shopping centers, regional malls, and large office parks.

PLATE 5

comparing
state**futures**

348
MILLION METRIC TONS (MMT)

*284 MMT

TOTAL CARBON EMISSIONS

5,600
SQ MI

*5,300 square miles

LAND CONSUMPTION

27,200
MI

*24,400 miles

HOUSEHOLD VMT

21.5
BILLION GALLONS

*15.9 billion gallons

ANNUAL FUEL CONSUMPTION

147,000
GALLONS

*166,000 gallons

WATER DEMAND PER NEW HOUSEHOLD

$22,000

*$12,900

UTILITY AND AUTO COST PER HOUSEHOLD

*2005 (Existing)

LAND-USE MIX
- ■ sprawl
- ■ compact
- ■ urban

5
25
70

trend
The "Trend" future continues standard development patterns of the last forty years dominated by low-density suburban growth. This future also has few policies to address carbon emissions and does not project increased building or auto efficiencies.

PLATE 6

The State of California has studied the impacts of various land use and transportation futures through the year 2050 to accommodate an additional 20.5 million people and 6.6 million households.

POPULATION GROWTH

2010	39,000,000
2050	60,000,000

HOUSEHOLD GROWTH

2010	13,200,000
2050	19,800,000

DIFFERENCE

83 MMT

76%
REDUCTION WITH A 1.6 PERCENT INCREASE IN POPULATION

1,850 SQ MI

AREA MORE THAN
Rhode Island
PLUS DELAWARE

18,000 MI

EQUIVALENT TO TAKING
6.5 million
CARS OFF THE ROAD EACH YEAR TO 2050

6.5 BILLION GAL

350 billion
GALLONS SAVED OVER 45 YEARS—
EQUALS OVER 5 YEARS OF U.S. IMPORTS

66,000 GALLONS

94 million
ACRE-FEET SAVED OVER 45 YEARS—
OVER 15 TIMES SF BAY

$11,100

$11,000
PER YEAR SAVINGS WOULD COVER A $240,000 MORTGAGE (10% DOWN, 5% INTEREST)

green urban

The "Green Urban" future assumes a more compact, walkable, and transit-served development pattern. It also assumes that buildings will be 70 percent more energy efficient, cars will average 55 MPG, and utilities will be 50 percent green—a suite of policies now under consideration by state law.

10
35
55

PLATE 7

A good transit system has many layers, from local buses to bus rapid transit and streetcars, from light rail to subways and commuter trains. They all feed into and reinforce one another, and they all depend on walkable urbanism at the origin and destination. The quality of the interface from walking to transit, and from one form of transit to the other, is central to displacing car trips and is the greenest technology that urbanism provides.

The relationship among transit, urbanism, travel behavior, and carbon emissions is complex but can be summarized with one key quantifiable metric, vehicle miles traveled (VMT)—effectively, the amount we drive. VMT is determined by the number and distance of trips we take, and our "mode split"—the percentage of trips taken by various transportation modes such as walk, bike, car, carpool, or transit. Each household, depending on its location, income, and size, has an average VMT per year, which when combined with various auto technologies will generate its travel carbon footprint.

Many factors affect VMT, and there are many complex models that simulate the travel behavior behind it. For example, the modal split among auto, walk/bike, and transit is affected by location and level of transit service as well as how pedestrian friendly the streets are; the average length of each type of trip is affected by land use patterns and how closely destinations are located; the number of trips per day is affected by household size; and auto ownership rate is affected by household income and size (for more of the interdependent variables, see chapter 6). The most significant variables in all this are the walking and transit opportunities of urbanism, a compact development form, and land use patterns that bring destinations closer together.

The power of place over travel behavior is demonstrated by mapping VMT per household across a region. While averages always lead us to stereotypes, different environments across any region reveal dramatically different travel behaviors. For example, in the San Francisco Bay Area, a typical household in the Russian Hill neighborhood of San Francisco has an average VMT of 7,300 miles a year. This neighborhood averages only three stories but is dense by suburban standards; has a rich mix of shops, restaurants, and services within walking distance; and is a short transit ride from downtown. Its walk score (an algorithm that awards points based on the distance to the closest amenity in several categories) is 98 out of 100—as good as it gets.

The Rockridge neighborhood in Oakland was created as a streetcar suburb back in the prewar days of the Key Route Trolley system, which connected most of the Bay Area until 1948. It is filled largely with bungalow and small-lot single-family homes but has small apartment buildings at corners and a wonderful mixed-use main street along with a BART (Bay Area Rapid Transit) train station at its center. The average household there drives about 12,200 miles a year and has a walk score of 74.

Out in San Ramon, a low-density East Bay suburb without good transit connections, development patterns fit the standard sprawl paradigm, with isolated single-family subdivisions, strip commercial arterials, malls, and office parks. VMT for the average home there is around 30,000 miles a year, and the walk score is 46.[29]

So there is a four-to-one range in travel behavior over three neighborhoods in one region. They differ in density, mix of uses, walkability, proximity to job centers, and level of transit service. The density in Russian Hill is 62 units per acre, but home values are $555 per square foot. In Rockridge, the density averages 15 units per acre and values are $420 per square foot. Finally, in San Ramon, considered a very high end suburban community, the average density is 3.4 units per acre and the value averages just $320 per square foot.[30] The market itself is telling us that walkable places have value and, as a bonus, can reduce our carbon emissions and oil dependence. So desirable is the walkable neighborhood that a 2009 study found that in cities like San Francisco and Chicago, moving from a household with a city's median walkability to one at the 75th percentile would increase the unit's value by over $30,000.[31] The challenge, of course, is to create walkable places as authentic and beautiful as Russian Hill and Rockridge that are affordable.

The point is that all of these community-scale systems—whether power, water, waste, or transit—need urbanism to be effective. Urbanism is essential for the viability of community cogeneration systems and the savings they provide in energy consumption. Denser, mixed-use development can provide the open space, community parks, and riparian setbacks needed by ecological water and waste recycling systems. And, of course, transit depends on urbanism for its fundamental viability.

These community-scale systems built around urbanism are not intended to replace the emissions reductions of efficient industrial processes, renewables in our utility portfolios, or better fuel standards for our cars. It is just that those supply-side strategies alone will not take us far enough quickly enough—and they come at a large cost premium. The combination of transit-served urbanism and green technology at the community scale is essential to complete the picture.

All of this discussion boils down to some simple choices in community building. One alternative simply extends our current land use patterns, architectural types, everyday aesthetics, and civic habits. As one example of this, imagine a *room* with a low-hung ceiling, sealed windows, and fluorescent lights; within a *building* with a mirror glass skin, set behind a parking lot off a six-lane arterial; in a *zone* of commercial development making up part of a *suburb* of subdivisions, shopping centers, and office parks connected by a freeway to a *metropolis* of decaying inner-city neighborhoods, struggling first-ring suburbs, exclusive suburban enclaves, failing school systems, and underfunded civic programs. This would seem like a biased contrivance if it were not so commonplace.

The other choice involves a quality of place making we seem to have lost touch with. It could be described as a *room* with high ceilings filled with natural light and breezes; in a *building* wrapping a courtyard and lining a street; in a *neighborhood* with tree-lined avenues, village greens, and local shops; making up a part of a *city* filled with streetcars, public squares, parks, and cultural districts; providing the focus of a *metropolis* with a constellation of many varied towns and cities connected by transit, growing economic networks, cultural institutions, and social opportunity. This also may seem like a biased contrivance, but it has been realized in some significant U.S. metro areas.

In both models, each layer is interdependent and connected by deep-rooted economic, policy, and social systems. Each is a complex that cannot easily exist piece by piece but nests layer by layer into a self-reinforcing "whole system." Certainly, the future will be a mix of these two extremes, but the question is: in what proportions?

Just how much change in land use, technology, and place making we can tolerate is the topic of the next chapter. A look back over the past fifty years of development and urban form reveals just how dramatic the shifts can be—and what trends will direct future growth. The question then becomes how to shape a vision for our future and what will be the best balance of design standards, policies, technologies, and economies to bring it about.

Over the past fifty years the physical and social fabric of our lives has changed radically, and our kids' lives are a profound reflection of that change.

I moved from London to Coral Gables in Florida about fifty

years ago—and, like Dorothy in the *Wizard of Oz*, the world turned Technicolor. I arrived in a town developed by the great visionary George Merrick, a community that most would now call a Norman Rockwell fantasy. As a kid, I could ride my bike anywhere, school was a walk away, and all my friends were local. At age six, I had independence—no playdates or organized sports, just a friendly neighborhood of shady streets, corner shops, and play areas in every vacant lot. After school, we managed our own time, lived out our fantasies, and shaped our own social worlds. In the past fifty years, that has all changed. Both parents are out working, the local stores are gone, bike-safe streets are rare, and a foreboding fear of abduction has locked down every kid's life.

Of course, such changes are driven by more than physical design, but I believe the form of our communities and our social norms are linked, albeit in complex ways. Statistically, abduction rates on a per capita basis are no higher now than they were in the 1950s. But fewer parents are willing to let their kids go out on their own—they won't even let them play in a park without supervision. Fifty years ago, it was common for kids like me to explore the wilder environs, venturing into the rougher areas around the railroad tracks and canals for adventure. Now there is too much fear, fewer connections between neighbors, and fewer adults around who are seen as community guardians. The physical and social fabric of our lives has changed radically, and our kids' lives are a profound reflection of that change.

After World War II, the United States experienced a boom like no other in its history. In a short period, we transitioned from the Great Depression and war to unprecedented wealth. This transition occurred in the context of explosive growth and a uniquely American version of a suburban new world. The American Dream as we know it now was born in the 1950s and 1960s as we built our interstate highway system, perfected the subdivision, first developed shopping malls, and abandoned our cities. In this period, government not only subsidized the infrastructure of the suburbs and financed the housing but also paid for its zoning through a large federal grant program.[1] Our national identity and international cachet were inextricably tied to cars, suburbs, and all things new.

The energy crisis and recession of the 1970s were only a pause in the suburban juggernaut. The baby boomer generation soon returned to their ever-growing

McMansions and SUVs in the Reagan 1980s. By this time, any memory of our once-grand urban places and compact towns had completely fogged over. But by the 1990s, a new generation began to shift direction and sensibility. In their eyes, cities were not all bad and the gleaming new suburbs were starting to wear thin. As the suburbs mushroomed, congestion, crime, affordability, and the sheer size and monotony of it all started to breed doubt. People liked their suburbs but stopped supporting more of them. In the early 1990s, New Urbanism, with its proposals for alternative forms of growth, and NIMBYs ("not in my back yarders"), with their desire to stop any and all growth near them, seemed to emerge at the same moment and have been battling ever since. At the same time, the children of the boomers began returning to the cities, embracing urban life, and sparking revitalization and reinvestments—the yuppie (young urban professional) was born. By the turn of the twenty-first century, the yuppies' older empty-nester boomer parents started following them back to the city.

Now, cities are again on the ascendance, and urban places have gained in relative value throughout most regions. Left behind, the old first-ring suburbs and the most distant exurban locations are starting to lose value and market share. Nevertheless, our homebuilders kept right on with the next ring of subdivisions as the banks offered irresistible subprime loans to keep the inventory moving—until, in 2008, the housing market collapsed.

This cartoon urban history is of course simplistic, but understanding just how much our community and culture have changed since World War II shows just how much they can, and indeed will, change in the next half century. Over the past two generations, systemic changes have produced radical shifts in the nature and form of our communities. Each of the drivers—massive cultural realignments, world-changing new technologies, seismic demographic shifts, new economic structures, and profound environmental challenges—is a vast field of study unto itself. I will try to extract the key elements of each driver as it affects the way we have developed, and can develop, our cities and communities. In the end, the data highlights, first, how mutable our urban forms are, and second, how out of sync our current development patterns are with emerging social, economic, and environmental needs—in effect, just how much change is possible, imperative, and imminent.

Social and Physical Norms

For the past fifty years, North America has been experimenting with a radically new form of settlement: the auto suburb. We transitioned from a country of villages, towns, and cities to a country of subdivisions, malls, and office parks. In 1950, just 23 percent of the population lived in suburbs; now, more than 50 percent does.[2] We spread out. For example, from 1970 to 1990, the Chicago region expanded geographically by 24 percent while its population increased only by 1 percent, and such cities as Detroit and

Pittsburgh urbanized over 25 percent more land even while their population *shrank*.[3] We became a country dominated by cars within a landscape designed for them. Between 1960 and 2000, the average vehicle miles traveled (VMT) per year by each of us doubled.[4] We became a decentralized service economy rather than an urban industrial economy. In 1970, only 25 percent of jobs were in suburbs; by 2006, that share had grown to 69 percent.[5] And we became more segregated by age, income, and culture as well as by race. All of these shifts found physical expression in our development patterns—suburban sprawl and urban decay, diminished natural resources and lost history.

But just when auto suburbs became the norm, we began to outgrow their basic assumptions. Most significantly, we are no longer a country of nuclear families. Only 23 percent of American households are now married couples with kids at home, and less than half of these subsist on one income.[6] Now, perhaps tragically, the largest household type is made up of single individuals and single parents.[7] What's more, over the past fifty years, the number of women working has more than tripled.[8] The "stay at home mom" foundation of the suburbs is effectively dead, but the need for a parental chauffeur service has grown.

As the "Ozzie and Harriet" version of the good life faded, other fundamental changes came: the globalization of capital and labor, the growing dominance of an information economy, a decaying and increasingly toxic environment, the continued disintegration of inner cities, intensifying geographic segregation of income groups, and the near collapse of our faith in public institutions, to name just a few. We hear about these challenges every day but cannot seem to find a comprehensive response or a coherent vision of a unifying personal or collective future. Filling the void, politicians vacillate between scapegoating (blaming immigrants and big government) and Band-Aids (creating regulations that address symptoms rather than root causes). Most people respond by withdrawal or anger, cocooning in special interest groups and retreating to private communities.

Unfortunately, this cycle of withdrawal has been feeding on itself. The less we invest in high-quality public facilities and community services, the more we need to retreat into gated or distant suburbs—and the more we seem to distrust our government. The most dramatic manifestation of this is families with kids chasing higher quality schools in the suburbs. Only rich suburbs can afford to subsidize schools to a functional level, while public funding for urban schools has dropped along with income levels. Urban schools remain one of the main reasons even families who love living in cities move to the suburbs. And with the flight of the middle class, urban tax dollars have declined where they were most needed and disinvestment reinforced. In the end, such disinvestment in the public sector is a negative feedback loop.

This withdrawal from the public world of civic facilities, community, and urbanism has been well documented by sociologist Robert Putnam of Harvard. In his seminal work *Bowling Alone: The Collapse and Revival of American Community*, he concludes: "For the first two-thirds of the twentieth century a powerful tide bore Americans into ever deeper engagement in the life of their communities, but a few decades ago—silently, without warning—that tide reversed and we were overtaken by a treacherous rip current. Without at first noticing, we have been pulled apart from one another and from our communities over the last third of a century."[9] All the social engagement indicators have trended away from community involvement and commitment. We attend fewer public meetings, we sign fewer petitions, and we participate in fewer local organizations.[10] From philanthropy and union participation to bowling leagues and membership in community organizations, the decline is as dramatic as it is worrisome. The pattern of transformation is clear, but simple explanations are not. Have urban decay and sprawl been a cause or a result of this cultural migration away from the commons?

Not only have we become a less civically involved society, more isolated in our "communities of interest," but we have also become a more economically segregated and polarized society. In most regions, suburbanization has tended to isolate the poor in inner cities, the working class in first-ring suburbs, and the affluent in "favored sector" suburban zones. Call it suburban apartheid. Moreover, the economically diverse neighborhoods that once existed in cities, places where doctors and lawyers once lived side by side with the working poor, disintegrated as the middle class of all races and backgrounds moved to the suburbs. Sprawl reflected a seismic social redistribution at the same time that it was an unparalleled physical reordering.

Demographics, Health, and Mobility

In architecture, "form follows function" has been the mantra of modernist design. In urbanism, the equivalent might be "form follows demographics." The form of our cities and communities is ultimately shaped by demographic trends: age, household size, income, and culture, to name a few.

Take housing, for example. Over the past forty years, nonfamily households (basically singles) have grown from 18 to 32 percent, with single men actually doubling as a household type. At the same time, married couples with children slipped from 44 percent down to 23 percent. Over three quarters of our households are childless (no wonder our schools are suffering).[11] Popular among real estate developers are the needs of "empty nesters," a cohort not ready for retirement villages but no longer in need of a suburban yard. Overall, we live alone more, with the national average of 3.3 persons per household in 1960 falling to 2.5 in 2000.[12] This means that while the standard single-family home in an isolated subdivision was a good fit in the past, it no longer is the best lifestyle fit for many today.

While household occupancy was falling, ironically the size of our houses was growing. In 1950, the average size of a new home was 980 square feet, and now it is 2,350.[13] This increase in size is certainly a luxury, but one that, after the housing crash of 2008, seems to have been subsidized in unsustainable ways. In addition, this growth in size is tied to more and more remote locations, as people have accepted longer commutes to find larger, more affordable homes. From an energy standpoint, both home size and distance translate directly into greater carbon emissions, environmental impacts, and household expenses. From a cost-of-living standpoint, the long commutes more than offset the savings in home cost, but that calculation seems to elude both home buyers and banks.

The same radical shifts can be seen in our relationship to cars and driving. In 1960, we averaged just one car per house, and now we have 1.9, with the biggest increase coming in the 1970s.[14] In the 1960s, only 2.5 percent of households owned three cars; now it is up to 17 percent.[15] One fifth of homes had no cars in the 1960s, while that figure is now down to one tenth.[16] America has never been a paragon of transit use, or of walking for that matter, but just after World War II, when we still had our streetcars and trolleys as well as our Chevrolets and Fords, we drove about 11,100 miles per household, whereas today we drive 24,000 miles.[17] None of this is a mystery: as we spread out and became more car dependent, household costs climbed and our daily lives changed.

One startling, unintended consequence of our increasingly auto dependent lives has been our health. We walk less, produce more air pollution from cars, and have more auto accidents. In the past fifty years, the total miles driven annually in the United States increased from 718 billion to over 3 trillion.[18] Although we have made great strides in auto safety and emissions, accidents and air pollution are partly proportional to miles driven. A 2000 study attributed forty thousand premature deaths and $50–80 billion in health costs nationally to air pollution caused by autos.[19] Harmful auto exhausts may have been reduced through higher emission standards, but air pollution still remains a problem. Many metropolitan areas in the country still struggle to meet their air quality standards. In fact, more than half the U.S. population lives in counties with air quality concentrations exceeding healthy levels established by the U.S. Environmental Protection Agency (EPA).[20]

Over the years, auto accidents may have dropped per mile of driving because of safer vehicles, but they have actually risen per capita because VMT has grown faster than car safety has improved.[21] Currently, over forty thousand people are killed and 2.5 million are injured on our roads per year.[22] The medical costs that result exceed $164 billion annually.[23] Interestingly, traffic fatality rates are highest in exurban areas, not cities.[24] Contrary to the eleven o'clock news, if you combine deaths from traffic with crime rates, living in cities is actually safer on average than living in the suburbs.

The United States has experienced what now qualifies as an epidemic of obesity and obesity-related diseases, primarily diabetes. The Centers for Disease Control and Prevention (CDC) estimates around two hundred thousand to three hundred thousand deaths per year occur prematurely as a result of obesity-related illness.[25] Many causes underlie this epidemic, but most prominent are diet and lack of exercise. Some percentage of this statistic is related to lack of exercise caused by auto use. Between 1977 and 1995, the average amount that we walked per day fell 42 percent while our auto use increased at three times population growth.[26] Some studies now directly relate walkable neighborhoods to higher levels of physical activity and lower obesity rates.[27] In fact, the evidence is so clear that the CDC has issued recommendations that call for improved access to transit, mixed-use development, and investments in pedestrian and biking facilities as strategies to help counter obesity.[28] Considering air pollution, accidents, and obesity, the costs of our fifty-year experiment with auto suburbs must be measured not only in gas and road construction but also in significant impacts on our basic health.

Economic Transformations

Beyond these profound health, demographic, and social shifts, the economic and technical changes of the past two generations have been dramatic. Many have documented and decried the country's declining industrial base. In 1958, 45 percent of our jobs were in basic industries, and now only 22 percent are.[29] Meanwhile, white-collar jobs increased from 42 percent of total jobs to 61 percent.[30] Emergent is the digital economy, an age in which white collar workers dominate. This of course has painfully affected regions that lack a diversified economy, such as Detroit, Michigan, and Akron, Ohio. It has also affected blue-collar middle-class incomes and lifestyles, and therefore the kinds of neighborhoods that they can afford and maintain.

The land use expression of this economic transformation was a shift from urban factory sites to suburban office parks, and from heavy industry to sprawling light industrial zones. As a measure of this change, the country's energy consumption in the industrial sector has dropped 32 percent per capita since 1960. Meanwhile, energy consumption in office buildings (home of the white-collar worker) has almost doubled.[31] One opportunity presented by this shift is the possibility of reintegrating the workplace with residential areas. Noisy, dirty urban factories were a principal reason the middle class fled the city in the first place; now, in both city and suburb, the workplace can easily be integrated as part of walkable districts and neighborhoods.

This shifting economy had a depressing impact on many family and city budgets. Much has been written about the stagnation of middle-class incomes since the 1970s.

In fact, inflation-adjusted income for the median household has risen less than 1 percent per annum since 1973.[32] But, ironically, this stagnation has not had a big impact on land use patterns or housing densities. Houses, yards, and cars all grew bigger even though paychecks didn't. Perhaps this partly explains the housing bubble of 2008.

The way we spend money did change, however. In the 1950s, the average household spent 27 percent of its income on housing and 13 percent on transportation, for a total of 40 percent. For many low- and working-income households today, the combined expenditure now reaches 60 percent. In 2002, transportation on average had increased to 19 percent and housing costs had moved up to 33 percent.[33] The increase in spending on cars is, of course, a key reflection of our auto-oriented land use patterns. For many households, multiple car ownership has long since shifted from a luxury to a necessity.

Economically, these changes have had big impacts on the fiscal limits of our cities and towns. As David Rusk documents in *Cities without Suburbs*, inner cities and first-ring suburbs lost their economic base as the middle class and white-collar jobs moved to the suburbs. Racial tension and deteriorating school systems in the inner city exacerbated what became known as white flight. Such depopulation, disinvestment, and loss of tax base has been reversed recently in some cities, as high-tech jobs, urban pioneers, and new-middle-class professionals have moved back to urban centers.

But regardless of where the fiscal pendulum swings, these shifts highlight the need for economic strategies that work on a regional level rather than pitting city and suburb against each other. The successful metropolis depends on regional economic systems that share tax base as well as affordable housing, adequate transportation investments, viable schools, and accessible open space systems.

Perhaps the largest economic shift of the past fifty years has been the emergent global economy and its implications for cities and regions. As industrial production shifts to low-wage centers around the world, the United States' regional economies depend more and more on clusters of innovation, creative intelligence, and place-specific industry clusters. An educated workforce and regional forms that create vital urban environments, expedite transportation, and balance jobs and housing opportunities are key to a robust regional economy. Global competitiveness highlights the need for communities with amenities that will attract the creative, mobile, value-adding people who tend to drive the global economy. They typically have the freedom to choose where they live and work, and they commonly prefer a more urban lifestyle. This is another reason, even a mandate, for a rebirth of urbanism. As Richard Florida summarizes: "Place still matters in the modern economy—and the competitive advantage of the world's most successful city-regions seems to be growing, not shrinking."[34]

Energy Profiles

In parallel with these dramatic shifts in demographics, economics, and cultural norms, enormous shifts in our energy consumption patterns have occurred. In the United States, as is well known, we demand much more than our fair share of energy and resources—almost five times the global average. But, perhaps surprisingly, our total per capita carbon and energy totals have not changed much over the past fifty years. Since we adopted the auto suburb model of development in the late 1950s, our total energy consumption per household (including industry, utilities, transportation, and buildings) has remained almost flat, at about 850 million Btu per household.[35] The reasons are complex: we drive more but have more efficient cars; our houses are bigger but also more energy efficient; and, perhaps most important, we have saved a great deal of energy in the shift from an industrial economy to an information economy. But our population has doubled from 52 million households to 117 million in that time period, so our country's energy and carbon emissions have doubled—and therein lies the problem.[36]

Here are the breakdowns. The total VMT per household has doubled from around eleven thousand miles per home in 1960 to around twenty-four thousand today (so the total miles driven in the country has actually quadrupled).[37] But even with lax fuel standards and cheap gas, efficiency has partially kept up, so the total energy used for passenger vehicles increased only 20 percent per capita.[38]

In heating and cooling our houses, the story is similar. Even with larger homes, the total energy use per house is about the same. This is because the actual demand in the home dropped by 56 percent as we built more efficient buildings with more efficient appliances and equipment.[39] Unfortunately, this was offset by the fact that we use more electricity, which is dramatically inefficient. Remember, it takes about three units of energy burned at the power plant to deliver one at the house, so the added electric use canceled other, more efficient building practices.[40] The net result: per capita energy use for housing and transportation is only slightly greater than it was in 1960.[41]

Since the 1960s, we have seen a major realignment in the commercial building and industrial processes sectors. Industrial energy use has dropped dramatically, by about 30 percent. Meanwhile, the energy to light, heat, cool, and run commercial buildings has nearly doubled. This shift from an industrial to a white-collar economy, while increasing commercial consumption, has saved overall energy and emissions on a per capita basis; the net result (commercial and industrial) is a 15 percent reduction overall.[42] The end result of all this—housing, transportation, commercial, and industrial—is a doubling of our energy consumption and carbon emissions commensurate with the doubling of our population.

A smaller but growing element in our energy profile is air travel. At the same time that we decided to build freeways and auto-oriented communities, we also decided to build airports rather than intercity rail. Today, air travel is on average around five thousand miles per year per household.[43] The alternative—high-speed rail—could provide for intercity travel for less than one quarter the energy.[44] Just as with housing and transportation, this technology is part of a whole: subdivisions or neighborhoods, malls or main streets, freeways or transit, airports or high-speed rail.

The changes in the past fifty years have left the United States with unsustainable energy needs and a disproportionate share of the world's emissions: five times that of the average person on the globe. But this history shows that big shifts are possible and, in fact, inevitable. It also brings us to a point of reckoning regarding energy, climate change, and the way we shape our communities. Accommodating this challenge will involve developing a new economic perspective as well as new urban forms. While the future will be shaped by our history, demographics, economies, and culture, it will also be affected by the land use paradigms that shape our lives and expectations.

The reality is that we are long overdue for change. Our demographics will propel new housing needs; our economics will mandate the invention of a less costly form of prosperity; and our environmental impacts, by every current measure unsustainable, will propel new technologies. Certainly, there are profound barriers to change, including inertia, cultural norms, vested interests, and political stalemates. But innovation, ingenuity, and flexibility have always been deeply embedded in the American character. And as can be seen from the past fifty years, change is inevitable. The only question is what type.

Confronting climate change is a
little like the war on drugs; you can
go after the supplier—coal-fired
power plants—or you can pursue
the addicts—inefficient buildings
and suburban sprawl. Both will
be necessary.

Toward a Green Urban Future
Chapter 3

Somewhere in the mid-1980s, mankind crossed a critical line:

for the first time in human history, our collective material demands exceeded the capacity of the planet to support us with its regenerative biological income.[1] We are now consuming the earth's capital reserve at an ever increasing rate. We see this in the degradation of ecologies and biodiversity throughout the planet; we see it in climate change, increased species extinctions, collapsing fisheries, erosion from deforestation, and many other environmental costs. To understand the roots of these environmental challenges, the Global Footprint Network translates our collective energy, food, and material demands into land areas and then compares them to the quantity of productive land available on the planet. The results are surprising.

Global Footprint Network has converted our total energy demand into the forestland area needed to absorb its resulting carbon emissions and then summed it with all the cropland, grazing land, forestland, fishing grounds, and built-up areas required globally. Their analysis shows that over the past fifty years, on a per capita basis, we have become more efficient in all our needs but energy. Since 1961, per capita demand for croplands, forestland, grazing, and fishing areas has dropped over a third—a meaningful and encouraging improvement even if not enough to offset the doubling population. Meanwhile, the global energy demand for each person has increased fivefold. In 1961, we needed just 0.7 acre to absorb our per capita carbon emissions; now we need 3.5 acres. Given that the global population has doubled in this period, our total energy needs have increased tenfold.[2]

Meanwhile, the world's capacity to support us has remained relatively flat (it is a finite planet after all). Our demand moved from a total of 17 billion acres to 42 billion acres needed to fill our homes, plates, cars, and storage units. The bad news is that the globe's biocapacity to supply these needs is only 29 billion acres, and it is not growing.[3] There are many factors driving the acceleration in energy consumption, including expanding industrial process, poor building design, inefficient utilities, exploding private transportation, and consumptive lifestyles, to name a few. And for each driver, the way we shape our cities and towns will be formative to reducing the demands. The type of buildings we construct, the quantity of travel we need, the efficiency of our power distribution systems, and our daily lifestyles each depend on the kind of urbanism that individual countries, especially developing countries, choose.

history of
urbanism

BIRTH OF THE AMERICAN DREAM
1950s

The suburban American Dream as we know it was born as we began to build our interstate system, perfect the subdivision, and abandon our cities.

150,700,000
POPULATION
2.3
BILLION TONS OF CARBON

BUILDING THE INTERSTATE SYSTEM
1960s

Our national identity and international standing became inextricably tied to cars, suburbs, and all things new. And social unrest in our cities accelerated the suburban trend.

178,500,000
POPULATION
2.9
BILLION TONS OF CARBON

ENERGY CRISIS
1970s

The energy crisis of the '70s and that decade's recession were the first signal of problems for our foreign oil dependence and low-density land use patterns.

203,200,000
POPULATION
4.2
BILLION TONS OF CARBON

SUV SUBURBIA
1980s

The baby boom generation returned to their ever growing McMansions and SUVs with Reagan. By this time any memory of our once grand urban places and walkable towns had completely fogged over.

226,500,000
POPULATION
4.7
BILLION TONS OF CARBON

TURNING THE TIDE
1990s

A new generation began to shift direction and sensibility. Yuppies began returning to cities, valuing urban life, and sparking revitalization and reinvestments. New Urbanism arose to advocate mixed-use walkable development.

248,700,000
POPULATION
5.0
BILLION TONS OF CARBON

BACK TO CITIES
2000s

At the turn of the century empty-nester parents started following the yuppies back to cities. Throughout many regions urban places gained in relative value till the great recession of '08.

281,409,000
POPULATION
5.8
BILLION TONS OF CARBON

The Rise and Fall of Sprawl Fifty years of radical change have reshaped the American landscape. What was once a country of cities and compact towns became a collage of subdivisions, office parks, and malls. Recently some of our cities and more walkable suburbs have staged a comeback. At the same time, the first-ring suburbs and the most distant exurban locations started to lose value and market share. Nevertheless, home builders kept right on building the next subdivision, the banks offered irresistible loans, and the housing bust hit in 2008.

PLATE 9

changes in
households

Postwar America experienced a massive shift to the suburbs. Jobs came along too, just 25 percent in 1970 up to 69 percent today.

LIVING IN SUBURBS

23%

50%

As middle-class wealth increased, and even when it didn't, home size grew exponentially. As household size dropped, "move-up" homes became investments rather than necessities.

SIZE OF HOMES

980 SQ FT

2,350 SQ FT

Demographics shifted dramatically from nuclear families with kids to a more diverse population. Close to half of all households today are headed by singles.

COUPLES WITH KIDS

44%

23%

The double-income family became the norm, partly to cover growing expenses. Along with it came "latchkey" kids, as the stay at home mom disappeared.

NUMBER OF WOMEN WORKING

1

3

Since the '50s, we transitioned from a country of villages, towns, and cities to a country of subdivisions, malls, and office parks. In so doing we spread out; for example from 1960 to 1985 the New York region expanded geographically by 65 percent while the population increased by only 8 percent and in Cleveland the land area increased 33 percent while its population actually decreased 8 percent. Overall we live alone more, with an average 3.3 persons per household in 1960 falling to 2.6 in 2005.

PLATE 10

changes in
transportation

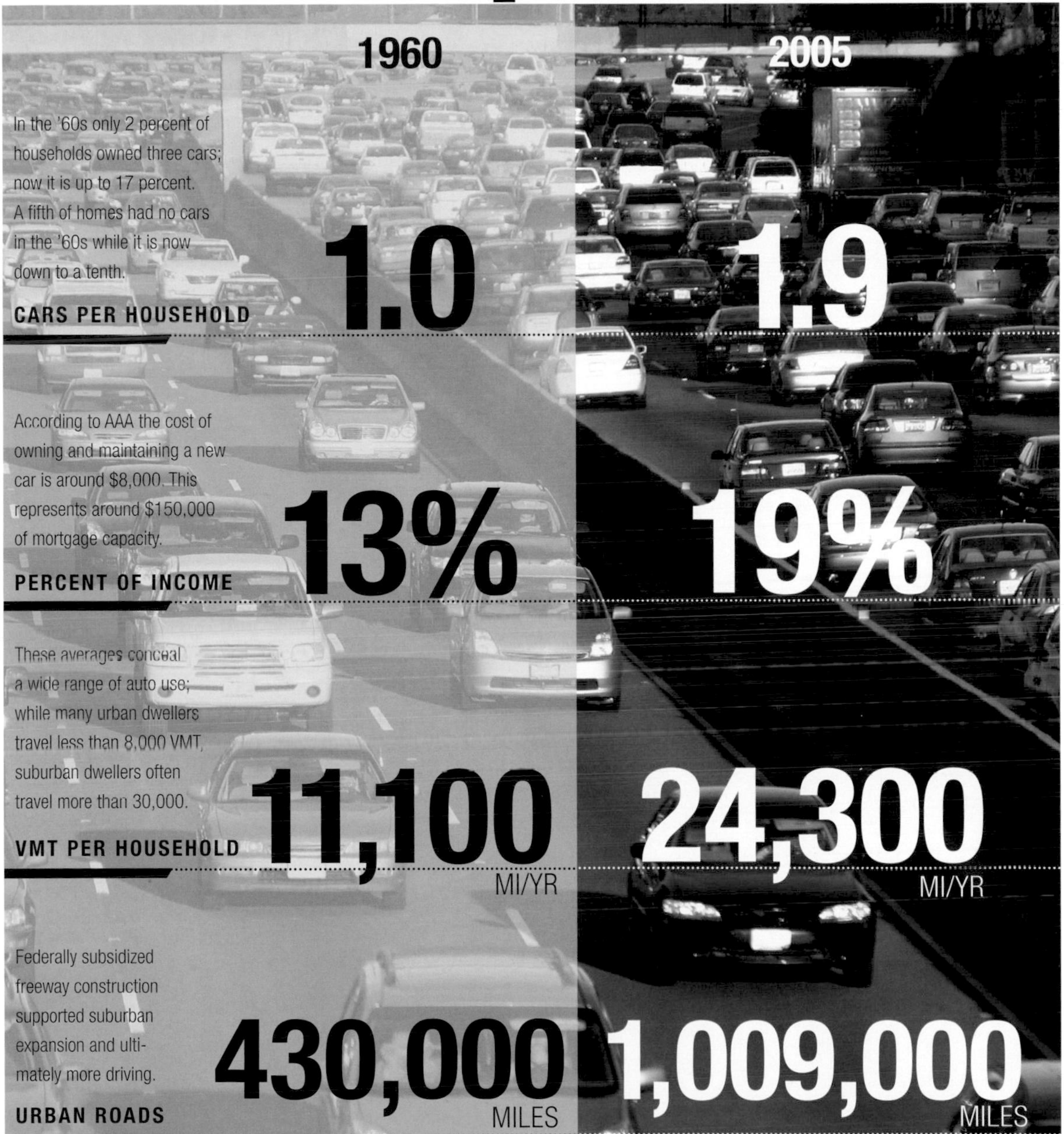

1960	2005

In the '60s only 2 percent of households owned three cars; now it is up to 17 percent. A fifth of homes had no cars in the '60s while it is now down to a tenth.

CARS PER HOUSEHOLD

1.0   **1.9**

According to AAA the cost of owning and maintaining a new car is around $8,000. This represents around $150,000 of mortgage capacity.

PERCENT OF INCOME

13%   **19%**

These averages conceal a wide range of auto use; while many urban dwellers travel less than 8,000 VMT, suburban dwellers often travel more than 30,000.

VMT PER HOUSEHOLD

11,100 MI/YR   **24,300** MI/YR

Federally subsidized freeway construction supported suburban expansion and ultimately more driving.

URBAN ROADS

430,000 MILES   **1,009,000** MILES

Our shift to an auto-based city has had many costs as well as benefits; the U.S. has never been a paragon of transit use, or walking for that matter, but just after WWII, when we still had our streetcars and trolleys, as well as Chevrolets and Fords, we drove half the miles that we do today, spent less on transportation, and had cleaner air.

PLATE 11

changes in
energy

1960	**178** million	
2008	**308** million	

U.S. POPULATION GROWTH

1960

2008

Even with lax fuel standards and cheap gas, efficiency has helped offset our increased travel so the energy demand for passenger vehicles per house increased only 20 percent.

262 MBTU PER HOUSEHOLD

311 MBTU PER HOUSEHOLD

TRANSPORTATION

10 trillion total

27 trillion total

The actual demand in the average home dropped by 56 percent because we built more efficient buildings. This was offset by the fact that we use more electricity, which is dramatically inefficient.

175 MBTU PER HOUSEHOLD

187 MBTU PER HOUSEHOLD

RESIDENTIAL

9 trillion total

21 trillion total

The shift to white-collar jobs and a service economy increased office space and its energy demands.

88 MBTU PER HOUSEHOLD

160 MBTU PER HOUSEHOLD

COMMERCIAL

4.5 trillion total

18.5 trillion total

Efficiencies and a profound shift away from heavy industry in our economy has cut our per household share of energy in this sector by a third.

400 MBTU PER HOUSEHOLD

270 MBTU PER HOUSEHOLD

INDUSTRIAL

20 total

31 total

As our number of households doubled from 52 million to 117, total energy consumption doubled from around 45 trillion BTUs to 100 trillion but surprisingly total energy used per household stayed about the same. We saved energy as we exported high energy industrial jobs overseas and increased efficiency in our cars and buildings. Transportation and buildings increased almost threefold in total while our use of electricity increased fivefold. Transportation is our fastest growing energy sector.

PLATE 12

changes in
carbon

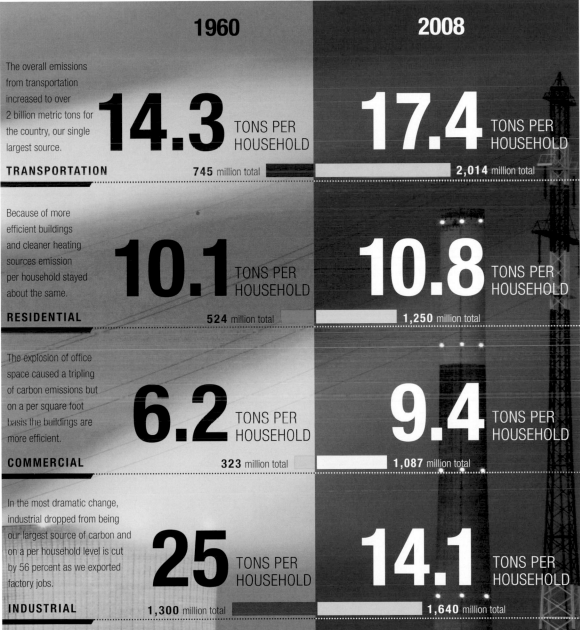

	1960	2008

The overall emissions from transportation increased to over 2 billion metric tons for the country, our single largest source.

14.3 TONS PER HOUSEHOLD
17.4 TONS PER HOUSEHOLD

TRANSPORTATION   745 million total   2,014 million total

Because of more efficient buildings and cleaner heating sources emission per household stayed about the same.

10.1 TONS PER HOUSEHOLD
10.8 TONS PER HOUSEHOLD

RESIDENTIAL   524 million total   1,250 million total

The explosion of office space caused a tripling of carbon emissions but on a per square foot basis the buildings are more efficient.

6.2 TONS PER HOUSEHOLD
9.4 TONS PER HOUSEHOLD

COMMERCIAL   323 million total   1,087 million total

In the most dramatic change, industrial dropped from being our largest source of carbon and on a per household level is cut by 56 percent as we exported factory jobs.

25 TONS PER HOUSEHOLD
14.1 TONS PER HOUSEHOLD

INDUSTRIAL   1,300 million total   1,640 million total

Changes in carbon emissions closely track energy consumption patterns. Transportation is now our most significant GHG source at over 2 billion tons and is increasing the most rapidly. Residential and commercial buildings come to more than another 2 billion metric tons and when combined with transportation represent the extraordinary opportunity of urbanism. Not listed here are the approximately 1 billion tons of noncarbon greenhouse gases produced by agriculture and chemicals.

PLATE 13

changes in the
ecologicalfootprint

	1961	2006
The explosion in transportation miles, electric use, and coal-fired power plants has increased the per capita lands required for carbon sequestration fivefold.	**3.00** ACRES per capita	**15.83** ACRES per capita
CARBON UPTAKE	567 million acres total	4,792 million acres total
A shift in U.S. diet toward fish doubled our demand for fishing grounds.	**0.22** ACRES per capita	**0.40** ACRES per capita
FISHING AREA	42 million acres total	119 million acres total
Increased demand for paper and wood expanded our forest demands.	**2.06** ACRES per capita	**2.90** ACRES per capita
FORESTLAND	390 million acres total	877 million acres total
Feedlots and corn based feed have reduced America's grazing lands for food. Free range meat is now a rare commodity.	**1.35** ACRES per capita	**0.16** ACRES per capita
GRAZING LAND	254 million acres total	47 million acres total
Higher productivity per acre through genetic engineering and carbon-based fertilizers has dramatically reduced our required croplands.	**6.69** ACRES per capita	**2.77** ACRES per capita
CROPLAND	1,262 million acres total	839 million acres total

U.S.

The Global Footprint Network finds that in the U.S. nonenergy land demands for food and materials have actually fallen on a per capita basis since 1961, from around 3.4 acres per person to 2.5. As we have exceeded the ocean's finite ability to absorb our carbon emissions, our net per capita impact has risen fivefold. In 1961 we needed just 3.0 acres to absorb our carbon emissions after ocean uptake; now we need 15.83 acres per person. As a result of our population's doubling and this increase in per capita emissions, our total energy footprint has grown close to tenfold.

PLATE 14

ECOLOGICAL FOOTPRINT BY SECTOR

- ▢ carbon footprint
- ▢ built-up land
- ■ fishing ground footprint
- ■ forest footprint
- ▢ grazing land footprint
- ▢ cropland footprint

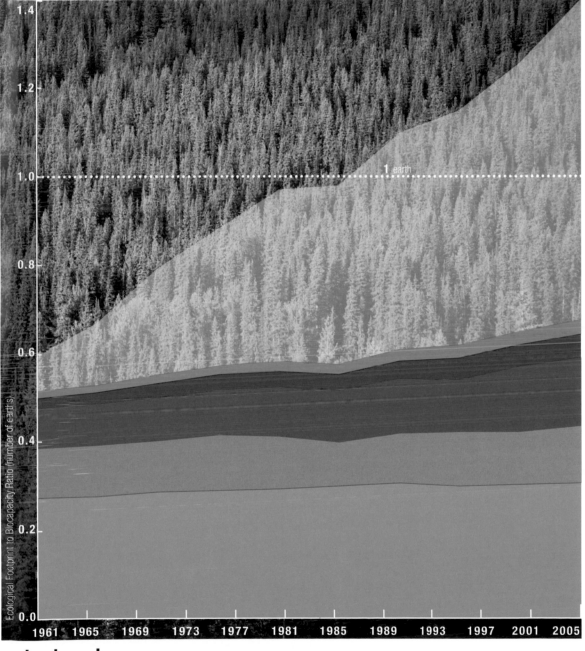

global The Global Footprint Network calculates the forestland area needed to absorb our total carbon emissions, then sums this land area with all the cropland, grazing land, forestland, fishing grounds, and built-up areas required by our population. The total—our ecological footprint—now exceeds the roughly 30 billion-acre biocapacity of the earth.

PLATE 15

By themselves, efficient buildings, high-mileage cars, and green technologies can and must play a central role in reducing carbon impacts. But that will not be enough. To achieve the 12% Solution, we will have to take 10 gigatons of carbon out of our economy by 2050, cutting our total to just 2.5 gigatons total greenhouse gas emissions. Of that amount, urbanism plus efficiency in cars and buildings can deliver over 4 gigatons of savings. The other part involves integrating green technology and renewable sources of energy within an urban future.

First Steps

Given the size and inertia of our political and economic structure, systemic change is always challenging. Entrenched interests, no matter how dysfunctional, are always resistant to shifts in norms, standards, or policies. This is normal; but perhaps less typical is a culture that has grown to expect standards of living to forever rise and consumer costs to always fall. Since World War II this has been the case, largely because of cheap energy, growing productivity, and technological innovation. In the 1950s, the average household spent 70 percent of its income on what were then deemed essentials (clothes, food, and shelter), while in 2003 spending on essentials dropped to 50 percent.[9] Simultaneously, consumer activity grew while savings and investments in infrastructure fell. If the shift to a low-carbon future depends on maintaining these attributes of high consumer spending and low infrastructure investments, change indeed will be difficult, if not impossible. In fact, the foundation of successful transformation will involve significant new infrastructure investments, changing consumer patterns, and the research and development to produce new technologies.

Most agree that we cannot shift to a green economy without pricing carbon higher, both to depress its use and to support investment in alternative green energy sources. Herein lies the political challenge; rich countries like ours are loath to pay more for current services or a quality of life they have grown to enjoy and expect, and poor countries lack the funds to cover any increased costs regardless of need. Conservatives claim that a carbon tax, or even a cap-and-trade system, would depress the economy by increasing costs and would therefore lead to job losses.

Progressives argue that we are giving more than the equivalent of such a tax to rich, oil-producing states and that we should at least keep the dollars here. They claim it is also reasonable to assume that, after a relatively short transition, renewable energy costs would come down and the new technologies would lead to an economic expansion based on "green jobs." This may be so, but getting there will be politically problematic. As always, sequence, speed, and degree of change matter in the political world. At this moment, a carbon tax does not seem to be a viable political option for addressing the climate change challenge in the United States.

However, a great deal can be accomplished without increasing energy costs across the board. Three interconnecting strategies for reducing carbon emissions and energy demands—urbanism, increased building efficiency standards, and higher auto gas mileage—can be put into place without a carbon tax or even cap-and-trade systems. These three strategies are needed in any viable future, and they produce many long-term benefits and actually save money. Urbanism and conservation are products of new design standards and intelligent planning, not new taxes or even new technologies. These policies alone would get us 40 percent of the way to our 2050 goal.

The well-respected McKinsey & Company cost/benefit analysis of 2007 "Reducing U.S. Greenhouse Gas Emissions: How Much at What Cost?" studied over 250 carbon abatement policies, technologies, and strategies and identified a large number that saved money over a relatively short period—good investments by any measure, regardless of carbon emissions. The overall conclusion was that the United States could do its part to stabilize the climate at little to no net cost to the economy. In fact, the study showed that the economic benefits of conservation alone could pay for the clean energy investments needed in our industrial and agricultural sectors.[10]

To simplify and clarify McKinsey's extensive range of options, the Natural Resources Defense Council (NRDC) grouped them into eight categories, from building and transportation efficiency to renewables, carbon capture, and "other innovations." The total savings from the range was over 10 gigatons of GHG—enough to get to the 12% Solution.[11] Some of the groupings are key complements to urbanism—increased building efficiency standards, higher auto gas mileage, and low-carbon fuels—and according to their analysis would result in over 4 gigatons of savings. What's more, each of these strategies pays for itself. For example, building efficiency would actually save forty lifecycle dollars for each ton of carbon abated. While the McKinsey or NRDC study does not calculate the costs/benefits of urbanism because the study precludes any behavior changes, it is clear that urbanism's reduction in auto dependence saves in gas and carbon while it reduces costs. Urbanism is the missing cost-positive carbon reduction strategy from these studies.

Let's look at the economics of each of the three major strategies—urbanism, building efficiency, and low-carbon autos—in a little more detail. Urbanism is a growth pattern that many in the real estate development industry see as the market preference for the next generation regardless of environmental needs. Future demographics and housing affordability challenges set the stage for a shift to higher density and more urban lifestyles. The Urban Land Institute (the country's foremost real estate developer organization) and PricewaterhouseCoopers have for years been projecting a growing market segment for New Urbanism, Transit-Oriented Development, and more urban infill in their annual report *Emerging Trends in Real Estate*: "Next-generation projects will orient to infill, urbanizing suburbs, and transit-oriented development. Smaller housing units—close to mass transit, work, and 24-hour amenities—gain favor over large houses on big lots at the suburban edge. People will continue to seek greater convenience and want to reduce energy expenses. Shorter commutes and smaller heating bills make up for higher infill real estate costs."[12] Nonetheless, we have continued to build new communities as if all families were large and had only one breadwinner, as if land and energy were endless, as if another lane on the freeway would end congestion, and as if we could afford anything through the alchemy of creative finance.

In fact, it is apparent to many that our urban forms need to be rebalanced to fit with today's culture, economics, and demographics. These new market forces need only be supported by rational changes in the zoning codes and a shift in our transportation investments to realize the potential of urbanism. On many levels already documented in the Vision California study discussed in chapter 1, this future would cost less for American households, cities, and businesses while increasing our standard of living and general health. Urbanism is a win-win strategy that comes without new taxes; in fact, it can ultimately reduce household, local, and state costs.

Building efficiency standards are also a win-win in that they ultimately decrease operating costs as well as emissions. Most building energy conservation strategies have a payback of less than five years. This means that, with the right financing, these improvements can be made without a cash-flow burden because reduced utility bills pay for the increased capital costs. A proof of this concept in general is California's Title 24 building standards. These building efficiency standards (along with those for energy-efficient appliances) have saved homeowners and businesses more than $56 billion in electricity and natural gas costs since they were adopted in 1978.[13] It is estimated the standards will save an additional $23 billion by 2013.[14]

Another example of the kind of program needed is the Architecture 2030 strategy to finance building retrofits and set aggressive new national building efficiency standards. Led by Ed Mazria, a pioneering passive solar architect in the 1970s, the 2030 Challenge sets new building emissions on a sliding scale moving to net zero emissions by 2030. The program allows 20 percent of the building energy to be provided by green utility sources or purchased as a carbon offset, so the effective standard for the building itself would be 80 percent lower than current design standards. This is a powerful and aggressive goal, but one that can and should be met.[15]

In addition, Architecture 2030 is advocating a federal program to weatherize existing buildings that provides lower mortgage rates in exchange for investments in retrofits that reduce energy consumption by 50 to 75 percent. Because of the reduced mortgage rates, homeowners would end up paying less per month while the retrofits would improve the value of their real estate. This retrofit program not only would reduce carbon emissions, limit the need for new electrical power plants, and reduce household utility bills but also would create up to nine million new jobs. Politically, this is a strategy that is hard to oppose.

In the end, increasing energy costs over the next forty years will mean that efficient buildings will be worth more. Owners will be paying significantly less in utility bills while experiencing increased real estate values and reduced operating expenses. We cannot get to the 12% Solution without more efficient buildings, but doing so will save us money and provide us with more comfortable environments.

The third strategy involves aggressive vehicle mileage standards. The auto industry in the United States has resisted shifting to more efficient vehicles and the federal government has been reluctant to set aggressive standards. More than industry, utilities, and buildings, autos are dependent on unstable foreign oil. The documentation about peak oil—the proposition that new oil reserves will peak and then diminish in proportion to rising worldwide demand, resulting in increased costs—is growing more and more convincing. But even without peak oil, exploding demand generated by a growing global auto fleet in emerging economies will no doubt drive gas costs dramatically upward. Abroad, especially in developing countries, more efficient vehicles will come to dominate the market. If the U.S. auto industry does not keep up with this market for efficient cars, further decay of the industry is certain. Establishing aggressive targets, such as the Pavley bill in California, will ensure that the U.S. auto industry will be at the cutting edge of this trend and will perhaps expand its global market share.[16] Such a policy, like building efficiency standards and support for urbanism, will strengthen the U.S. economy while it reduces fuel costs for average citizens, reduces foreign oil dependence, and cuts our carbon emissions.

Urbanism, along with auto and building efficiency standards, is the low-hanging fruit in the orchard of remedies to the climate change challenge. All three are politically easy to accomplish because they do not depend on increased energy pricing and they provide many co-benefits: lower household costs, preservation of more open space, more vibrant cities, more competitive industries, and a healthier population, to name only a few.

However, while urbanism, building efficiency, and increased MPG provide the essential foundation for change, they alone will not be enough. The emissions from industry, agriculture, and electric utilities also need to be reined in. Those sectors are more dependent on price signals and will need cap-and-trade legislation or carbon taxes coupled with subsidies. Unfortunately, these policies represent a higher political hurdle and are commonly misrepresented as job-killing taxes. As a result, much of the discussion around climate change is framed as an expensive economic shift rather than a welcome set of investments that save money for both households and government. We should start with the rewarding policies of urbanism and efficiency standards and build from there.

The Economics of Urbanism

Many argue that addressing climate change will cost too much for our economy, government, or personal budgets. They claim that limiting carbon will become a hidden tax and that more environmental regulation would render us uncompetitive in the global marketplace. But in the arena of urbanism, the results may be not increased costs but immediate savings. Unlike many renewable energy sources, more compact development patterns are a carbon reduction strategy that costs less than its alternates today. These cost savings are manifest at both the household and municipal level.

Historically, low-cost, low-density housing was available at the metropolitan fringe. People would trade growing commutes for affordable single-family homes. But if one looks at the combined costs of transportation and housing rather than at just housing mortgage, utilities, and property taxes, a different perspective on affordability emerges. What was thought of as a low-priced house in the exurban hinterlands becomes relatively expensive. And, conversely, a close-in home at a higher sales price can be less burdensome on the household pocketbook after factoring in travel costs.

The mismatch between the cost of sprawl and household economic capacity is camouflaged because we do not have a full accounting. Between 10 and 25 percent of a household's budget is spent on transportation—auto ownership, insurance, maintenance, gas, and parking.[17] As gas prices increase, so does this critical segment of every household budget. Keep in mind that our existing gas tax covers only about half the cost of road construction and maintenance; the other half is covered by general taxes. Housing affordability will further erode as the incremental price of road maintenance, improvements, and construction is added to the cost of new housing through development fees and local taxes. In addition, these costs do not include the burden of time lost to longer commutes and congestion. Finally, deferred environmental impacts are beginning, through government regulation and mitigation requirements, to filter down to the consumer's checkbook in other ways. In sum, the economics of sprawl are collapsing—in fact, they collapsed as of the housing bust of 2008.

The "location efficient mortgage" captures this underlying reality by combining the cost of housing with the cost of transportation. Developed by the Center for Neighborhood Technology, it advocates a higher rate of financing for homes that are located in places that reduce transportation costs—allowing the homeowner to spend transportation savings on their mortgage rather than on longer commutes, more cars, and more gas. Effectively, they can invest more of their money in a sometimes appreciating asset—their home—rather than an always depreciating asset—a car.

In many regions of the country, the most affordable single-family homes are the most distant from key job centers. These remote suburbs average a higher number of cars per household and greater travel distances. The average three-car household spends close to $13,300 in auto ownership, maintenance, gas, and insurance; a two-car household, around $8,900; and a single-car home (which was the average back in 1960), about $4,450.[18] According to AAA, owning and operating a new car is estimated to cost around $8,000 per year.[19] The savings of not owning that car applied to a home mortgage would finance about $125,000 of home value.[20]

In addition to the increased transportation cost associated with low-density development, there are also increased infrastructure costs. Many "costs of sprawl" studies over the past few decades have documented this. They calculate many factors and provide for complex trade-offs, the most elusive being the comparative cost of infill and redevelopment sites. The hard costs of new developments at the metropolitan fringe, however, are easy to quantify, and the economic comparison is dramatic. The cost of providing local roads and utilities for low-density growth over what can be two to three times the land area for more compact alternates is a relatively simple linear relationship. We have found repeatedly in our regional plans that these simple hard costs end up between $20,000 and $30,000 more per household for large-lot subdivisions when compared to more compact mixed-use growth. That leaves aside the increased operating expense of extending public services, such as police, fire, school bus, and emergency response. There is also the additional capital expense of developing new water and energy sources for the less efficient land use patterns.

A good example of such a comparison was developed for a new growth area in southeast Fresno in the Central Valley of California, romantically called the Southeast Growth Area. Here, forty-two thousand new homes were reconfigured on just half the land originally zoned, resulting in a saving of over nine thousand acres of prime farmland. This smaller footprint was the result not of a radical change in lifestyle but of simply a shift from large-lot single-family to more standard, small-lot and townhome building types. In addition, the new, more walkable community design and mix of uses resulted in transportation savings for each home of over $7,000 per year. The more compact building forms saved another $1,000 annually in energy costs. As a societal bonus, carbon emissions were down 50 percent overall and water consumption was down over 60 percent. The more compact alternate was still "suburban" living but in a format that actually provided housing types and sizes that better matched the market needs.[21]

While the numbers for low-density growth versus compact development in new areas are easy to calculate, the trade-offs for infill and redevelopment are more complex. This is because infill costs are highly variable, depending on unique reconstruction needs, variable expansion of existing utilities, and the additional time and money typically needed for permits. The cost of basic infrastructure for low-density greenfield development versus infill redevelopment is therefore hard to generalize. But, in most cases, the cost of upgrades and mitigations of infill is less than that of extensive, new low-density developments. And the annual savings of infill locations near jobs and transit remains a significant advantage for the individual homeowner.

This all brings us to the problems of affordable and workforce housing along with first-time home buyers—all growing market segments of the home building industry. Strategies for creating such housing often trend toward subsidies, cheap and distant land, density bonuses, special financing, and lower construction quality. But each of these strategies has problems. Affordable housing on cheap land isolates the poor, subsidies are scarce, density is anathema to many neighborhoods, creative financing is limited, and construction quality is already cut to the bone. Solutions can no longer come only from the mindset of cutbacks and subsidies. A broader picture of how we form communities and how we see the home itself is central to rethinking this chronic economic problem.

Affordable housing must start with affordable neighborhoods, affordable life-styles, and affordable infrastructure. Imagine a neighborhood in which transit was within walking distance and ran frequently. Where one could stop on a short walk at a daycare center, favorite shop, bank, health club, or café. Where the streets were tree lined, free of sound walls, and free of speeding cars—a neighborhood in which some trips could be made conveniently on foot, transit, or bike. Think of a neighborhood in which a three-car family could be a two-car family, or a two-car home might choose to have only one. Imagine a place in which driving was an option rather than a necessity. A neighborhood in which the money spent on the driving and the car could be used for mortgage or rent. And where the time spent in the car could be traded for time in the community, with the family, or reading on the train. For a struggling family, the benefits of these economies can be profound.

Affordable housing in this form is rare largely because of public policies rather than economic limits or market forces. We choose to subsidize highways rather than transit and in so doing commit the working poor to own several cars. We choose to make building mixed-use neighborhoods difficult because of single-use zoning and mortgage underwriting standards. In addition, many communities blatantly practice exclusionary zoning by establishing minimum lot-size requirements or simply by lim-iting new construction. Changing these policies and practices not only will begin to resolve some of our affordable housing problems but also can break the logjam of traffic congestion, deteriorating air quality, and loss of open space—and help respond to the climate change challenge. These are integrated solutions for complex intercon-nected problems. And they are just one example of the many ways an environmentally sustainable future can also be affordable and socially robust.

But the issue of gentrification must be addressed along with a much hoped for middle-class migration back to the city and other urban places. In some places of extreme poverty, diversifying the local population is a good thing; mixed-income neighborhoods typically bring enhanced public services, more convenient retail, and better schools. But displacing whole communities without an appropriate mix of affordable housing is a mistake. In fact, gentrification may be the biggest structural problem with urban reinvestment, as the very goals and benefits of revitalization often mean the displacement of poor residents, unless there are public programs to prevent and compensate for the dislocation. It's a chronic and vexatious problem that the free market is not able to address. The greatest challenge for inner-city TOD, or any inner-city redevelopment, is to balance the need for affordable housing with the need to diversify the city with economically integrated communities. Each place will go through a painful but necessary process arriving at this balance.

More inclusive suburbs can ease urban gentrification. More affordable housing at transit-rich suburban locations can not only provide needed alternatives for inner-city poor but also bring needed workforce housing near employment centers throughout the region. Many suburban towns cannot even provide housing that is affordable to its own teachers, police, fire, and other service workers. In an average U.S. household, 34 cents of each dollar spent is on housing and 17 cents on transportation. For some lower income households, the cost for both housing and transportation reaches 60 cents of every dollar.[22] For these working households, affordable housing that puts them close to transit in job-rich sections of the region is essential to making ends meet. However, TODs may theoretically cost less to live in, but if they become desirable and there are too few of them, the price will inevitably rise.

Barriers to Change

Along with these economic pressures, the global imperatives of climate change, peak oil, habitat loss, and resource depletion have refocused our society on energy consumption and environmental stewardship. But this is not the first time. The oil embargo of the early 1970s foreshadowed our current deeper and more complex challenge. That moment passed, and its single-issue focus was lost. But many other issues arose to make us rethink our patterns of settlement—the cost of housing, loss of open space and farmlands, growing traffic congestion, the fiscal vulnerability of our towns, the impact of digital technologies on everyday life, and the loss of community life and social capital in our cities. When a design does not work in one dimension, chances are that it is failing in others. In many ways, our modern land use patterns and the 1950s version of the American Dream are fraying—if not dying.

We all sense that sprawl as a dominant pattern of growth has become more and more dysfunctional. In fact, it has come to produce environments that frustrate rather than enhance everyday life. Yet, addressing these deficiencies seems to elude us even as their burdens grow. This is largely because the pattern's problems surface as what seem to be isolated issues: traffic congestion, lack of affordable housing, pollution, lack of time, the health effects of air pollution, and the fractured quality of our communities. In addition, sprawl's paradigm and assumptions are so powerful, so much an a priori, that most people think the solutions to these problems are just more of the same—more highways to cure congestion, more subdivisions to provide affordable housing, and more gated enclaves to stave off pollution, crime, and loss of community. The sprawl model is so powerful that its only antidote seems to be to replicate itself.

Confronting climate change is a little like the war on drugs; you can go after the supplier—coal-fired power plants, for example—or you can pursue the addicts—inefficient buildings and suburban sprawl. In fact, to succeed, both tactics will be necessary: renewable sources for power generation as well as conservation in buildings; fuel-efficient cars as well as land use patterns that reduce the need for cars. To do this, we need both short- and long-term structural change in land use and energy sources. Short-term solutions turn to efficient cars and retrofitting buildings. Long term, we need an urban landscape filled with fewer cars and more elegant, climate-responsive buildings.

If our settlement patterns are the physical reflection of our culture, then—like our society—they are clearly becoming more and more fractured. Our developments and zoning laws segregate age groups, income groups, and ethnic groups as well as family types. Increasingly, they isolate people and activities in an inefficient network of congestion and pollution. Our fundamental sense of commonality, essential to any vital democracy, is seeping away in suburbs designed more for cars than for people, more for market segments than for communities. Special interest groups have now replaced citizens in the political landscape, just as gated subdivisions have replaced neighborhoods. The social, economic, political, and environmental need for systemic change is obvious.

Part of the challenge lies with the fractured professions in charge of directing growth. We have specialists (architects, traffic engineers, landscape architects, civil engineers, planners, and so forth) for all the individual elements of community design but no profession to put the pieces together, to look after the synergies and think through the trade-offs. The result manifests the bias of specialization—a suburban landscape that can easily be seen as an ill-fitting collage of separately designed enclaves, each optimized for its own needs but with little vision of the whole. The same is true in public policy. Each government department (whether housing, transportation, health, education, or environment) develops policies that often overlook the possibilities of integrated solutions and the tragedies of unintended consequences. Comprehensive policies, integrated professions, and whole systems design must be the foundation of systemic change.

Unfortunately, integrated solutions are also frustrated by the structure of our governance and the scale at which we make decisions. We have piecemeal planning at the local level complemented by stovepipe planning at the state and federal level. Until recently, the problems of open space preservation, affordable housing, highway congestion, air quality, and infrastructure costs were treated independently by separate agencies and institutions, as if there were no linkages. In addition, policy makers persisted in treating the symptoms of these integrated problems rather than addressing the development patterns at their root. We control air pollution with tailpipe emissions, fuel consumption with more efficient engines, and congestion with more freeways—all rather than simply making cities and towns in which people are less auto dependent. Treating both symptom and cause is now essential for real and meaningful change.

The barriers to such change are significant. Foremost is the weight of plain old inertia, the comfort of the known. Urbanism, with its compact and mixed-use communities, often seems alien and a menacing Trojan horse for low-income populations, different lifestyles, and decreasing property values. This bias is amplified by a sense that any "new" development—even more of the same—will diminish the quality of a place rather than enhance it. And for decades, typical suburban development has done just that; each new project has increased traffic, reduced open space, overtaxed services, and polluted the environment. When growth means more of the same, it is no wonder people oppose any development, especially infill close to their homes. The sad result is that development leapfrogs to virgin land at the metropolitan fringe, where newer communities welcome the construction jobs and where government too often underwrites the infrastructure.

If such resistance to infill is the "push" of sprawl, then the "pull" is the dream of life closer to nature, privacy, and escape from the city. There is no doubt that for those who can afford it, a large house on a large lot with several big cars is a very comfortable lifestyle. And given modern media, who needs direct access to the culture of the city? Chris Leinberger, in *The Option of Urbanism*, gives the most concise list of sprawl's allure: privacy and land, affordable homes due to low-cost construction and federal tax deductions, communities filled with similar people, better public schools, relative safety, and free parking.[23] These items have all been very attractive for decades, but now they have been compromised by another list: congestion, suburban crime, loss of open space, smaller lots, rising taxes, declining services, decaying infrastructure, increased commuting costs, and, worst of all, parking meters. The "pull" of new sprawl has lost its glitter as well as its affordability. To top it all off, the climate change implications of more sprawl are becoming apparent to all who are willing to look at the numbers.

To conclude, the economic limits of our current patterns of growth are now painfully apparent on many levels. The true environmental and health costs of climate change, air pollution, imported oil, overtaxed resources, and lost open space may be deferred but never fully avoided. Beyond these pressing environmental impacts, the economics of our current development patterns are hard to sustain for many working families. The soaring costs of transportation, services, infrastructure, and housing all raise questions about the viability of a land use pattern that is affordable only to a diminishing percentage of the population.

More and more, the costs of auto-oriented development cannot be absorbed by the average new home buyer, by local government, or by the environment. The housing bust of 2008 should be seen as clear evidence of the unsustainable costs of sprawl compounded by a significant shift in the housing market as well as by the excesses of overextended credit.

The good news is that setting a low-carbon direction in land use policy is synonymous with changes that can ensure the economic, social, and ecological health of our cities and towns. Unlike changing lightbulbs or installing solar panels, redirecting land use patterns can accommodate a broad array of agendas, goals, and needs. There are many technical fixes that enhance our capacity to limit greenhouse gas emissions, and they must be pursued vigorously. But urbanism, though it offers one of the most potent long-term antidotes to climate change, cannot turn on this need alone. Indeed, to meet the challenge of climate change—to rebuild an economy that is sustainable and equitable—involves nothing less than redesigning the American Dream.

Against the modernist design philosophy of specialization, standardization, and mass production stands a set of principles rooted more in ecology than in mechanics. These are the principles of diversity, conservation, and human scale.

Design for Urbanism
Chapter 4

Too often we plan and engineer rather than design. Planning
tends to be ambiguous, leaving the critical details of place making to chance, and
engineering tends to optimize isolated elements without regard for the larger system.
If we merely plan and engineer, we diminish the possibility of developing a design that
makes informed trade-offs between isolated efficiencies and integrated parts. Design
is multidimensional problem solving, while engineering is single-issue optimization.
Both are necessary, but at this stage of development Bucky Fuller's whole systems
design is what is needed.

The engineering mentality typically reduces complex, multifaceted problems to
one or two measurable dimensions. For example, traffic engineers optimize road size
for auto capacity and speed without considering all the other elements of good streets,
such as neighborhood scale, walkability, natural habitat, safety, or beauty. Civil
engineers efficiently channelize our streams without considering recreational, ecological, or aesthetic values. Commercial developers optimize for market value and the
delivery of goods without balancing the social need of neighborhoods for local identity
and meeting places. Again and again, we sacrifice the synergy of the whole for the
efficiency of the parts.

The idea that communities should be designed rather than engineered or planned
is central to urbanism. The typical expectation is that we should plan a framework
and engineer the pieces, and let the rest emerge. The common impression is that our
neighborhoods, towns, and regions evolve organically (and somewhat mysteriously)—
that they are the product of powerful but invisible market forces or the summation of
technical imperatives. There is also the illusion that these forces cannot and should
not be tampered with—that engineering is good for the parts, and the invisible hand
of the market, with little if any regulation, takes care of the rest. Anything else is a
form of socialism and should be avoided at all costs. This view has brought us not only
communities that are less than the sum of their parts but ones that are increasingly
bankrupt and plagued by the housing bust of 2008.

Historically, urban design played a large role in shaping our forms of settlement.
The template that underlies much of our suburban growth was designed in the 1930s
by Frank Lloyd Wright with his Broadacre City and by Clarence Stein in his Greenbelt
New Towns. These ideas were then bastardized and codified by the U.S. Department
of Housing and Urban Development's minimum property standards in the 1950s and

by Federal Housing Administration (FHA) financing regulations. Le Corbusier and a European group of architects called Congrès Internationaux d'Architecture Moderne (CIAM) developed the template for city development about the same time. Their rationalist vision of superhighways, superblocks, and high-rise apartments, as well as their disdain for the traditional street and mixed land uses, became the basis of our postwar urban renewal programs and much of Soviet bloc housing policies. These flawed and ultimately failed models have reinforced the sense that urban design is dangerous—it failed in the past and is therefore doomed to fail in the future.

We need to move beyond the specialization of engineers and the vagaries of planning to rediscover the art and science of urban design. It is an art because cities are inherently about human narratives, about compromise and contingency, and it is a science because analysis and empirical evidence must be respected and utilized. The challenge is grand: urban design must integrate the work of all the single-minded specialists; it must balance economic, social, and environmental needs; and it must in the end create places that are beautiful, memorable, and convivial. A good urban designer must be part artist, part scientist, part historian, part futurist, part architect, part engineer, part planner, and part politician. To do this, urban designers need a unifying ethos to underpin community design.

A New Design Ethos

The problem is not only that our suburbs and cities lack design, but that, since World War II, they have been designed according to the wrong paradigm, based on failed principles and flawed implementation strategies. Specifically, our communities have been designed according to modernist design principles and implemented largely by specialists. The core modernist principles of specialization, standardization, and mass production were drawn from an industrial paradigm. When translated into a design philosophy, they had a devastating effect on the character and sustainability of our neighborhoods, cities, and regions. These three principles displaced generations of urban design wisdom with a radical experiment that reshaped our cities and towns as "machines for living" rather than civic frameworks for community. The modernist canon quickly came to dominate the world of planning, architecture, interior and industrial design—and the world we now live in.

In planning, the term *specialization* has multiple meanings. First was that each aspect of community design should be isolated and professionalized. Civil engineers, traffic engineers, environmental scientists, economists, landscape designers, and architects, as well as bankers, realtors, and appraisers, each came to control their own standards, codes, and policies—to command literally separate areas of our community land use maps. Each area within the map was matched by a parallel department in government. Hence the complex multiuse agendas historically layered into our streets, public spaces, and even buildings devolved into simplistic single-use zones. This principle of specialization even had an effect at the regional scale; it came to mean that each city or town could play an independent and economically isolated role. Suburbs were for the middle class and new businesses; cities, for the poor and declining industries; and countryside, for nature and agriculture. No mixing was allowed, no synergies, no shared responsibilities, and little complexity.

As a complement to specialization, *standardization* led quickly to the homogenization of our communities, a blindness to history, and the demise of many ecological systems. A "one size fits all" mentality of efficiency overrode the unique and often irreplaceable qualities of place and community. The subdivision, with its identical housing models; the shopping center, with its generic format; and the office park, with its uniform building type, all became standardized marketing and financing packages that varied only in superficial style across the country. Chris Leinberger, a real estate developer and visiting fellow with the Brookings Institution, has identified a total palette of only nineteen development types that make up the universe of financeable land use packages—all as reductionist as a Monopoly board.[1] And, of course, such standardization was necessary for underwriting the securitized debt that went on to undermine our whole economy during the 2008 financial crisis.

Mass production (in housing, transportation, offices, and so forth) upended the delicate balance that once existed between craft, local enterprise, regional identity, and global networks. The logic of mass production moves relentlessly toward ever-increasing scales, which in turn reinforces the specialization and standardization of everyday life. Efficient mass production, like standardization, ignores the unique qualities of history, local ecology, and cultural identity. It contributes to a loss of human scale, of local identity, and ultimately of any sense of place that is authentic or grounded.

Against this modernist alliance of specialization, standardization, and mass production stands a set of principles rooted more in biology than in physics, more in ecology than in mechanics. These are the principles of diversity, conservation, and human scale. *Diversity* is at the core of any robust, rich ecology; *conservation* means that nothing is ever lost in natural systems and that there is no such thing as waste; and *human scale* is nature's tendency toward detail and complexity. In urban design, diversity implies more mixed, inclusive, and integrated communities. Conservation implies the care for and recycling of existing resources—whether natural, social, architectural, or institutional. The principle of human scale brings the individual back into a built environment that has been increasingly shaped by remote and mechanistic concerns.

Moreover, these ecological principles apply equally to the social, economic, and physical dimensions of communities. For example, the social implications of human scale may mean police officers walking a beat rather than hovering overhead in a helicopter; the economic implications of human scale may imply development policies that support small local business rather than national industries and corporations; and the physical implications of human scale may be realized in the form and detail of buildings as they relate to the street and the pedestrian. Unlike the isolated governmental categories of economic development, housing, education, and social services, each of these design principles brings together physical design, social programs, and economic strategies. These principles, then, should form the foundation of a new urban design ethic.

Human Scale

Human scale is a design principle that responds simultaneously to simple human desires and the emerging ethos of decentralized economies. The focus on human scale represents a shift away from top-down social programs, from command-and-control organizations, from uniform housing projects, and from bureaucratic and remote institutions. Human scale in economics means supporting individual entrepreneurs and local businesses. Human scale in community design means a walkable neighborhood focus and an environment that encourages everyday face-to-face interaction. In its most concrete expression, human scale is the stoop of a townhouse or the front porch of a home rather than the stairwell of an apartment or the garage door of a tract home; it is a walkable city block rather than an auto-dominated superblock; it is local and decentralized services and nearby destinations rather than remote public and private institutions—it is the fine grain of great urban places.

For several generations, the design of buildings, the planning of communities, and the growth of our institutions have exemplified the view that "bigger is better." Efficiency was correlated with large, hierarchical organizations and processes. Now, the idea of decentralized networks of small entrepreneurial groups and more personalized institutions is gaining currency in both government and business—"small is beautiful" is popular again. Efficiency is correlated with nimble, small working groups, not large institutions. The same is true for the urban environment.

Certainly, today's reality is a complex mix of both of these trends—human scale and "bigger is better." For example, we have ever-larger big box retail outlets at the same time that main streets are making a comeback. Some businesses are growing larger and more centralized while the "new economy" is bursting with small-scale start-ups, intimate working groups, and virtual firms. The range of housing types is diversifying at the same time that production is consolidating into larger, more homogenous financing packages. Both trends are evolving at the same time, and the shape of our communities will have to accommodate this complex reality.

Yet people react negatively to the current imbalance between these two forces. The building blocks of our communities—schools, local shopping areas, housing subdivisions, apartment complexes, and office parks—have all grown into forms that defy human scale. And we are witnessing a reaction to this lack of scale in many ways. People long for an architecture that puts detail and identity back into what have too often become generic and mundane buildings. They desire the character and scale of a walkable street, complete with shade trees and buildings that orient frequent windows and entries their way. They enjoy, even idealize, main street shopping areas and historic urban districts.

The shape of a street, ironically even when lined by high-rises, can be human scaled if its storefronts are varied and interesting, if its entries are frequent and rich in detail, and if its edges are filled with human activity. Small local parks may not be efficient to maintain, but they support community and walkability in ways that are essential to healthy neighborhoods. Likewise, small schools, especially for elementary and preschoolers, are scaled to the emotional and social needs of children and fit into communities in ways that larger institutions cannot. Community-scaled technology, such as small, dispersed electric power plants coupled with district heating systems, can be thought of as a human-scale alternative to large centralized power plants. Finally, the small human-scaled buildings that accommodate start-up and local businesses are often at the heart of a vibrant, creative economy.

Diversity

Diversity has multiple meanings and profound implications. In nature, diversity is the key to resilience and adaptive capacities within any ecosystem. In community design, diversity has overlapping layers of physical, economic, and social meanings. Physical diversity results in maximizing the mix of activities, building types, and civic places within a community. Economic diversity tends toward places that support a broad range of businesses at differing scales. Social diversity produces places that are integrated and inclusive. As a planning axiom, diversity calls for a return to mixed-use neighborhoods that contain a rich range of uses as well as a wide choice of housing types for all economic, ethnic, and age groups.

The four fundamental components of any community—civic places, commercial uses, housing opportunities, and natural systems—define the physical dimensions of diversity at any scale. As a physical principle, diversity in neighborhoods ensures that destinations are close at hand and that the shared institutions of community are closely integrated. It also implies a varied architecture rich in local character and streetscapes that change with place and use. It is the antithesis of the "one size fits all" approach to housing, workplaces, and public buildings.

As a social principle, diversity is controversial and challenging. It implies creating neighborhoods that provide for a large range in age groups, household type, income, and race. Commonalities have always defined neighborhoods, even if they are energized by differences. But today we have reached an extreme: age, income, family size, and race are all divided into discrete market segments and constructed in separate locations. Complete housing integration may be a distant goal, but inclusive neighborhoods that broaden the economic range, expand the mix of age and household types, and open the door to racial integration are feasible and desirable. The success of the HOPE VI program to replace single-income federal housing projects with mixed-income communities is a dramatic demonstration that this principle can be realized even at our social extremes.

Diversity is a principle with significant economic implications. Gone are the days when economic revitalization efforts focused on a single industry or a major governmental program. A more ecological understanding of industry clusters has emerged. This sensibility validates the notion that a range of complementary but differing enterprises (large and small; local, regional, and global) are important to maintaining a robust and sustainable economy, and that now more than ever quality of life and urbanism play a significant role in the emerging economy.

Finally, diversity is a principle that can help guide the preservation of local and regional natural resources. Clearly, understanding the complex nature of stressed habitats, ecologies, and watersheds mandates a different approach to open space planning. Active recreation, agriculture, and habitat preservation are often at odds. Just as in the built environment, diversity in the range and type of natural areas within a metropolitan area is essential. A broad range of open space types, from the most active to the most protected, must be integrated in community and regional designs. Diversity in use, diversity in population, diversity in enterprise, and diversity in natural systems are fundamental to a sustainable future.

Conservation

Conservation implies many things in community design in addition to husbanding resources and protecting natural systems; it implies preserving and restoring the cultural, historic, and architectural assets of a place as well. Conservation certainly calls for designing communities and buildings that require fewer resources—less energy, less land, less waste, and fewer materials—but it also implies caring for what we have and developing an ethic of reuse and repair, in our physical and social realms as well as natural landscapes. Restoration and conservation are more than environmental themes; they are an approach to the way that we think about community at both the regional and local levels.

Conserving resources has many obvious implications in community planning. Foremost is the opportunity to save the farmlands and natural systems displaced by sprawling development and the voluminous auto travel it requires. Even within more compact, walkable communities, conservation of resources can lead to new design strategies. The preservation of waterways and on-site water treatment systems can add identity and natural amenities at the same time that they improve water quality. Energy conservation strategies in buildings lead to designs that are climate responsive while reinforcing a unique identity of place.

Conserving the historic buildings and institutions of a neighborhood helps to preserve the icons of community identity. Restoring and enhancing vernacular architecture can simultaneously reduce energy costs, reestablish local history, and create jobs. Although the preservation movement has made great strides with landmark buildings, they are now wise in extending their agenda beyond building facades to the social fabric of neighborhoods and the economic ecology of the communities that are the lifeblood of any historic district.

Conserving human resources is another implication of this principle. In too many of our communities, poverty, lack of education, and declining job opportunities lead to a tragic waste of human potential. As we have seen, communities are not viable when concentrations of poverty turn them into a wasteland of despair and crime. In this context, the term *conservation* takes on a larger meaning: the stewardship, restoration, and rehabilitation of human potential wherever it is being squandered and overlooked. There should be no natural or cultural environments that are disposable or marginalized. Conservation and restoration are practical undertakings that can be economically empowering and socially enriching.

These three principles—human scale, diversity, and conservation—set the foundation for a new direction in community design. Sprawl and its regional structure are a manifestation of an older and markedly different paradigm: the industrial qualities of mass production, standardization, and specialization. As a counterpoint, the principles and concurrences of human scale, diversity, and conservation define a new paradigm for the next generation of growth, one that leads from sprawl to sustainable communities. These principles need to be expressed at the scale of local community and the regional metropolis. Regional design is beginning to emerge as a key to our economic, social, and environmental health. It can be guided by the same urban design principles that work for neighborhoods and towns.

Region and Neighborhood

An interesting set of parallels emerges when regions and communities are designed according to the principles of human scale, diversity, and conservation. Each principle has meaning and specific design implications at both the regional and neighborhood scales. First and foremost, the region and its elements—the city, the suburbs, and their natural environment—should be conceived as a unit, just as the neighborhood and its elements—housing, shops, parks, civic institutions, and businesses—should be designed as a unit. Treating each element separately is endemic to many of the problems that we now face. Just as a neighborhood needs to be seen as a whole system, the region must be treated as a cultural and economic ecosystem, not a mechanical collage of isolated places.

Seen as this integrated whole, the region can be designed in much the same way as we would design a neighborhood. That the whole, the region, would be similar to its most basic element, neighborhoods, is an important analogy. Both need protected natural systems, vibrant centers, human-scale circulation systems, a robust civic realm, and integrated cultures. Developing such a design approach for the region creates the context for healthy neighborhoods. Developing such community design for the neighborhood supports regions that are sustainable, integrated, and coherent. The two scales have parallel features that in fact reinforce one another.

Major open space corridors within the region, such as rivers, ridge lands, wetlands, or forests, can be seen as the "village green" at a metro scale—as the commons of the region. These natural commons establish an ecological identity as the basis of a region's character. Similarly, the natural systems and parklands at the neighborhood scale are fundamental to its identity and character. A neighborhood's open space, like the region's, is as much a part of its commons as are its civic institutions and commercial centers.

Just as a neighborhood needs a vital center to serve as its crossroads, the region needs a vital central city to serve as its cultural heart and link to the larger economy. In sprawl, both types of centers are failing as remote discount centers and relentless commercial strips overcome what were historic town centers with human scale. In the central cities, poverty and disinvestment erode historic neighborhoods as the central business district decants jobs to dispersed suburban office parks. Both fall prey to specialized enterprises oriented to mass distribution rather than the local community. Like our natural and civic "commons," these urban and suburban centers are fundamental to local and regional coherence.

The design of regions and neighborhoods has other parallels. Pedestrian scale within the neighborhood—walkable streets, easy bikeways, and nearby destinations—has a mirror in regional transit systems. Transit organizes the region in much the same way a walkable street network orders the neighborhood. Transit lines focus growth and redevelopment in the region just as main streets focus a neighborhood. Crossing local and metropolitan scales, transit supports the life of pedestrians and bikers within each neighborhood by providing access to regional destinations. In a complementary fashion, pedestrian-friendly neighborhoods support transit by providing easy access for riders. The two scales, if designed as parallel strategies, are codependent and reinforce each other.

Diversity is a fundamental design principle for both the neighborhood and the region. A diverse population and job base within a region supports a resilient economy and a rich culture in much the same way that diverse uses and housing in a neighborhood support a complex and active local community. The suburban trend to segregate development by age and income translates at the regional level into increasing spatial and economic polarization—the "secession of the successful," as Robert Reich articulated in *The Work of Nations*.

These parallels across scales are not mere coincidence. The fundamental nature of a culture and economy expresses itself at many scales simultaneously. Shifting our fundamental postulates from a mechanical to an ecological paradigm will therefore manifest at every level.

Regionalism Emerging

We are in the embryonic stage of regionalism, still testing different approaches, ideas, and implementation strategies. In the past two decades, a significant range of regional designs, policies, and legislation has evolved in several states across the country. One lesson is already clear from these early trials; there is no one solution or process. In each place, variations in history, size, ecology, geography, economics, and politics have caused different forms of regionalism to develop.

It is important to remember that there are already many regional institutions coordinating critical infrastructure, investments, and policy—but in a piecemeal fashion. Regional transportation investments are controlled by metropolitan planning organizations (MPOs) as part of the process of allocating state and federal money for transportation and infrastructure. But they have little control over the land use patterns that drive these demands. Other single-purpose regional entities have evolved to deal with unique regional assets. A good example is the San Francisco Bay Area's Bay Conservation and Development Commission, which controls development along and in the bay. But land use remains the singular domain of local jurisdictions and is at the heart of the greatest controversy surrounding regionalism.

Effective regionalism does not imply that each town gives up land use control. Board policies, goals, and infrastructure criteria can be established at the regional scale that local governments can then develop and implement through their comprehensive plans and design codes. The region, in cooperation with local governments, can establish goals and policies in several general areas, including preservation of regional open space systems, efficient infrastructure configurations, the location of major job centers, significant transportation investments, and fair-share housing goals. Within these regionally set parameters, each local government can design a unique plan for growth that defines all the elements of their community: housing, circulation, open space, land use, and urban design.

In fact, without such regional policies, many local initiatives are frustrated. For example, without regional support, individual towns may be unable to preserve the open space systems they desire. And, clearly, the major transportation improvements each city needs can be developed only at the regional level. In fact, land use decisions must be adopted at the local level while coordinated at the regional level.

Oregon and Washington provide two alternate approaches to regional policy, design, and public participation. In Oregon, a more top-down approach was implied in the creation of a regional government with district elections for local representation. This governing body has primary responsibility for a regional Framework Plan that sets overall growth, infrastructure, and land use policies, as well as the placement of an urban growth boundary (UGB). Contrary to popular belief, the UGB in Oregon was not created to limit growth or stop sprawl; rather, it was enacted to protect farmlands from destabilizing land speculation and the resulting high taxes. The 1972 legislation called for a boundary that would always allow for a twenty-year supply of developable land and for periodic line adjustments to accommodate growing demand. Prior to a 1992 regional visioning process, called Metro Vision 2040, the overly elastic UGB had little effect on suburban growth or urban form. Vision 2040, in adjusting the UGB, asked if the region should "grow up" or "grow out" and involved considerable community input. Given the choices and the trade-offs, the plan to "grow up" with more compact forms of development was selected by a wide public margin.

The significant aspect of Oregon's growth management law is not that a top-down regional bureaucracy should dictate land use to local governments, but that the area must analyze the impacts of future growth at a regional scale and come to a comprehensive decision as to what direction to take. When allowed to see clearly the impacts of sprawl on their quality of life, the cost of infrastructure, and the impact to the environment, a majority of citizens opted for a more compact, transit-oriented growth pattern. These are trade-offs and choices people can make only when shown the cumulative impacts and costs of different forms of growth at a regional scale.

In Washington state, the process started with –rather than resulted in—such a regional visioning effort. The 2020 Vision produced a plan that configured the Seattle region with a hierarchy of "centers" and a complex set of growth boundaries that respected the needs and aspirations of individual communities. The plan was so successful that it led to state legislation for growth management. Under Washington state's Growth Management Act, the local governments remain the proactive force in land use decisions, with the regional entity setting overall direction and acting primarily as a board of appeals. Each local government was to develop a plan to accommodate its allotment of development and establish a local UGB. Local decisions can be challenged for either unreasonably breaching a locally imposed UGB or undermining the general allocation of jobs and housing within each community. In other words, environmentalists have recourse if a district begins to sprawl beyond its growth boundary, and developers have recourse if NIMBYs constrain appropriate levels of development within the boundaries.

Maryland's approach under Governor Parris Glendening provides a third model. It regulated land use through economic efficiency standards for such public investments as highways, sewer, water, housing, schools, and economic development assistance. Rather than prescribing the location and pattern of development, the state's Neighborhood Conservation and Smart Growth Initiative limited the state's investments in infrastructure to "priority funding areas." The concept was not to control the market or constrain private property rights but merely to spend public dollars cost effectively. Significantly, the priority funding areas were designated by the county governments, not the state. The areas, however, must meet several standards, such as minimum density and coherent infrastructure plans, along with accommodating the demonstrated need for growth. Land outside the priority areas can be developed but only at the local government's or property owner's expense. In this approach, the state seeks fiscal efficiency and the private sector develops areas that are market wise. State-subsidized sprawl is curtailed.

In addition, Maryland had several other programs to protect open space and encourage job growth in existing centers. Its Rural Legacy Program used sales tax dollars and bonds to purchase conservation easements on critical open space and farmlands. This program acknowledged that some lands would not be protected by the priority area designations and that in certain important areas additional measures are reasonable. The Job Creation Tax Credit program provided tax benefits to employers who created jobs in the priority areas, and the Live Near Your Work program offered home-buying assistance in areas in which the employers were willing to provide matching assistance. The goal was to create more compact, efficiently served communities while preserving the state's open space and farmlands. The means were a sophisticated mix of incentives and limits. But underlying it all is the notion that, without state and federally subsidized infrastructure, sprawl will wane.

Most of these programs ended in Maryland as political power shifted in the state. But the concept of a state husbanding its resources by targeting infrastructure expansions to cost-effective areas makes sense. In part, this has been a longstanding policy in the Twin Cities of Minnesota through their urban service boundary policies—a strategy to limit water, sewer, and road infrastructure to areas where growth makes sense.

Sometimes a nongovernmental, bottom-up approach works. In Salt Lake City, an initiative led by a civic group, Envision Utah, created alternative growth scenarios for the fast-growing area. These scenarios to accommodate the next one million in population ranged from a compact, transit-oriented alternative of 112 square miles of new development to a sprawling 439 square miles. The infrastructure cost difference between the extremes was extraordinary—close to an additional $30,000 per new home. In addition, the low-density option did not meet the market demand for multifamily housing or affordable lots for first-time home buyers. This low-density option reflected a growing trend in the region's smaller suburban towns toward an exclusionary zoning that allocated residential land primarily for large-lot single-family homes.

Envision Utah showed that taken piece by piece, individuals tend to oppose denser development, but when shown the cumulative loss of open space, affordable housing, and the additional tax burden caused by sprawl, their response can be quite different. A mail-back survey included in the local newspaper describing the Envision Utah alternatives showed that only 4 percent of the respondents preferred the trend low-density growth alternative while over 66 percent voted for the more compact alternatives.

In addition, the respondents voted in similar proportions for more walkable forms of development with increased transit investments. The most preferred alternate matched the market demand for multifamily and small-lot homes while reducing the average lot size of a single-family home by about 20 percent. This option also placed three fifths of the new residents within half a mile of planned rail transit stations and advocated mixed-use neighborhoods that made walking convenient in 70 percent of the new developments.

Since this effort was launched, the state passed the Quality Growth Act. Like the land management approach in Maryland, this legislation puts into place a commission to designate "smart growth" areas that will become the focus of new development and redevelopment. These areas will have state and federal priority for new infrastructure and services. Other areas, although not specifically outside of a UGB, will have to pay their own costs of development without public subsidies.

To date, the region has been aggressive about implementing the Quality Growth Act. Its new light rail line opened to ridership levels that exceeded projections, its downtown is experiencing a renaissance, and many suburban towns are competing for transit extensions by planning for TODs. One of the region's most successful developments, Daybreak by Kennecott Land, which was planned for twenty thousand new households, has demonstrated that compact, mixed-use, walkable communities sell well in a region that has historically been wedded to large-lot subdivisions. In fact, in the four years since its opening, Daybreak has been the top-selling community in Utah.

Most important for each of these approaches is their recognition that a definitive regional plan is a necessary precondition for the kind of urbanism described here and that citizen participation is a key to its success. When given clear information and a picture of the aggregate impacts of piecemeal, fragmented growth, most citizens opt for very progressive policies, even in historically conservative areas. This involves a critical shift in perspective: seeing growth in terms of its total impacts rather than one project at a time. Regional challenges get different responses than local questions.

A new taxonomy of mixed-use places will replace the old pattern of single-use zones—neighborhoods replacing subdivisions, village centers replacing shopping centers, and town centers replacing office parks and malls.

The Urban Footprint
Chapter 5

Translating the design principles of traditional and green urbanism into practical standards for development involves rethinking the basic building blocks of the region and its jurisdictions—creating a new armature of circulation along with a new language for zoning and planning. In the end, our transportation system will shift from autocentric roads and highways to a finer-grained, more connected network that provides for the pedestrian, bikes, and transit as well as autos—what are now called "complete streets." Likewise, our approach to planning will shift from segregated single-use zones to a rich, finer-grained lexicon of mixed-use places and communities. Rather than the simplistic land use designations found on most zoning maps today, diverse "place types" are needed to design complete regions, cities, and towns. There are five basic categories of such a place-based approach to community design: neighborhoods, centers, districts, preserves, and corridors.

Neighborhoods are the most basic building block of community. They are, by definition, walkable areas that integrate a range of housing with parks, schools, and local services. *Centers* are the mixed-use destinations of a group of neighborhoods; they include jobs and housing as well as services and significant retail. *Districts* are special-use areas typically dominated by a primary land use, such as a university, a cultural center, or an airport. *Preserves* are the open space elements of the region, be they productive agriculture, parklands, or natural habitat. *Corridors* are the edges and connectors of the region's centers, neighborhoods, and districts. They come in many forms, from roads and highways to rail lines and bikeways, from power-line easements to streams and rivers. Maps that use variations of these five simple elements can help us to reconceive and redirect planning at the regional and local levels.

Neighborhoods

The subdivision is the most ubiquitous product in the American landscape—a cluster of houses isolated by arterials and often unified by income, age, and building type: a community of likenesses rather than a community of diversity. A true neighborhood is much more complex—its definition is elusive and elastic and can take a wide range of forms, densities, and scales. In its simple physical ideal, a neighborhood is a walkable place with clear boundaries, shared parks and facilities, and an identifiable center of local services and schools. It includes a variety of people, offering housing opportunities for rich and poor, large family and small, young and old. Its diversity and human scale breed a kind of intensity and sociability that creates a resilient identity and a strong sense of community.

Many types of neighborhoods do not meet this ideal yet still sustain healthy communities. Some residential areas, for example, have several centers that are shared among neighborhoods. In truth, a neighborhood is less like a self-contained cell with its own isolated nucleus and more like a network of overlapping places and shared uses. It does not necessarily have a simple boundary or a single center. In fact, we now live in digital neighborhoods as much as physical neighborhoods, and the typical adult's social and economic lives are in many cases regional. Nonetheless, the idea of a local and physical neighborhood is essential for kids, seniors, and (I would argue) all of us—local friends and acquaintances as well as familiar shopkeepers and services ground us in ways that still are intrinsically important. At their best, neighborhoods offer a way of knowing and connecting to people who are not just like us.

We live in nested communities that telescope in scale, the most local being a walking radius that cannot (at anything less than the highest densities) provide for all of our daily needs. In most cases, our sense of neighborhood extends beyond to other destinations necessarily shared by several neighborhoods. And, certainly, the identity and range of a neighborhood shift for different people: whereas seniors and kids may consider the neighborhood to be a sharply defined area that they sense as "theirs," mobile adults may gather a larger area into what they would call a neighborhood. Everyone's mental map is not at the same scale.

Just as important as the physical context are the social, economic, and cultural networks that spring up in a neighborhood setting. These are the networks of daily life that produce what sociologists call "social capital." In the words of Harvard's Robert Putnam, who popularized the notion in the early 1990s, social capital consists of "civic engagement, healthy community institutions, norms of mutual reciprocity, and trust." Social capital broadens people's sense of self from "I" to "we" and encourages them to work together on community problems. Based on research, Putnam believes that community life—and even effective democracy—depends for its strength and vibrancy on the kind of informal networks that can be created only by a dense web of community organizations and neighborhood affiliations. With social capital, Putnam suggests, communities thrive; without it, they falter.

Putnam created a controversy in academic circles by suggesting that social capital in the United States was dramatically on the wane. As evidence, he pointed to a sharp decline in participation in community organizations of all kinds: churches, unions, parent-teacher organizations, the Elks Club, the League of Women Voters, the Red Cross, the Boy Scouts, and even—in the observation that gave Putnam's work its name—bowling leagues. In his book *Bowling Alone,* Putnam cites statistical evidence that Americans are far less likely to socialize with their neighbors than they formerly were.

Sociologists such as Putnam have been at a loss to explain just exactly why our nation's stock of social capital appears to be diminishing. Indeed, some have argued that there is, in fact, no loss of social capital at all. Rather, people simply associate with one another in different ways. Instead of bowling leagues, they create the informal networks required for social capital by engaging one another on the Internet. In other words, the argument goes, we don't need strong communities of place if we have strong communities of interest.

It is alluring to think that, thanks to the Internet and other virtual communication, ours can still be a society rich with social capital even if our neighborhoods disintegrate—if "face to face" no longer matters and the chance encounters no longer happen. But no matter how strong and powerful our chat rooms and Facebook networks become, it is hard to imagine that our metropolitan regions can be strong and vibrant if our neighborhoods continue to unravel. Robert Putnam recognizes this idea as counterintuitive: "My hunch is that meeting in an electronic forum is not the same as meeting in a bowling alley—or even in a saloon."[1]

Centers

Village, town, and city centers are the focal points, workplaces, and destinations of neighborhoods within the regional landscape. They gather together neighborhoods and local communities into the social and economic building blocks of the region. They are mixed use, combining housing of different scales with businesses, retail, entertainment, and civic uses. Such centers form the key job centers of the region. In addition to employment, each typically includes civic uses and public spaces, such as greens, squares, churches, government institutions, recreation facilities, and day care. At their best they have a walkable network of streets, human scaled and lined with accessible uses.

Centers are distinct from neighborhoods but may include neighborhoods. The distinction is that neighborhoods are primarily residential with some civic, recreational, and support uses mixed in. Centers, on the other hand, are primarily retail, civic, and workplace dominated with some residential uses mixed in. They are the destinations of several or many neighborhoods. Centers are also the appropriate location for major transit nodes and transfer points. They are, by definition, the TODs of the region.

A hierarchy exists from village center through city center, but there are no hard-and-fast distinctions among the types of centers, only general qualitative differences. In all cases, urban centers are qualitatively different than their modern replacements: shopping centers, malls, office parks, and industrial zones. Although many of these commercial developments name themselves village or town centers, these names are often an empty illusion. True urban centers are profoundly different. In addition to being walkable and mixed use, they are civic in ways that the parking lots and single-story boxes of our commercial environments can never be.

A village center is the most common and smallest of this type. Its retail component is defined by the inclusion of local stores, such as a grocery and pharmacy along with smaller shops and restaurants. A village center typically mixes second-floor uses—housing and small offices—with its retail. It adds recreation and civic uses and integrates all these activities within an accessible and walkable street system. It is typically a local destination for five to ten neighborhoods.

A town center is larger and more commercial than a village center. It typically includes a large number of office and employment uses, along with nighttime facilities, such as cinemas, theaters, museums, and hotels. Its retail component is close to the scale of what the retail industry calls a "community center," anchored by several major stores that are accompanied by specialty shops and restaurants. Second floor office and residential uses add to the intensity and urbanity of the area, and cinemas, bars, and restaurants maintain its nightlife.

The most important potential of the town center is as a subregional employment center and the potential for strong transit connections. Unlike the typical suburban format, its office buildings are not surrounded by parking lots and its uses are not separated by six-lane arterials. Parking is located to the rear, structured and shared with nighttime and weekend uses. The addition of significant housing also transforms these areas into more complex urban neighborhoods as well as regional destinations. This mix of uses and intensities makes the town center a key station in any regional transit system.

Defining a city center is complex and elusive as it can come in so many forms, densities, and characters. City centers are the most compact form of community with the greatest range of uses in the region. Even more than in a village or a town center, city centers must be mixed use, walkable, dense, and transit served. They must also be more intense, more inclusive, more diverse, and more active than their smaller regional counterparts. They hold the history, the color, the economics, and the cultural character of the region. As they become the cultural and economic focus of the region, they also become the transit vortex of the metropolitan circulation system.

Regions can and, in many cases, do have several city centers. For example, the San Francisco Bay Area has at least three: San Francisco, San Jose, and Oakland. Either multiple or singular, city centers form the primary focus of a region. They are the business, cultural, and civic centers that provide the global identity and international destination of a metropolitan area. They can be as different as Chicago, Portland, or Los Angeles, and those differences in turn help to define the surrounding metropolis.

Districts

Not all places in the new lexicon are urban or mixed. Districts are areas that accommodate uses not appropriate for a mixed-use environment—those that cannot be of a scale, mix, and character that fit within a neighborhood or a center. Examples of such uses are plentiful: light and heavy industrial areas, airports and major seaports, big box retail and distribution centers, military bases, and university campuses, to name a few. Districts are also the locale for LULUs (locally unacceptable land uses): the junkyards, abattoirs, auto repair shops, rail and truck depots, prisons, and so forth. These areas are critical to the economic and functional life of a region but must be separated from the fine grain of a neighborhood or the complex mix of a center.

Unfortunately, some uses that are often segregated as part of districts can be more closely integrated with centers—and should be. Office parks are a prime example. Under current zoning, these primary work destinations are isolated and clustered into single-use districts near freeway interchanges. Through some misplaced identification with factories, offices are too often seen as a poor fit with village, town, and city centers. To the contrary, they should be integrated into our mixed-use centers. Such integration adds strength to the retail, reinforces the transit system, and increases the value of any of the center's civic uses.

The challenge of integrating offices into urban centers is often their scale. The design challenge is to maintain human scale and pedestrian connections with large buildings and even larger parking areas. In city centers, the solution is conventional and well established: the high-rise building wrapped with ground-floor retail. In town centers, midrise buildings can be integrated into a block system that respects the pedestrian while allowing efficient building footprints. Shared parking, structured parking, and reduced parking (when transit is accessible) all can help mitigate the separations typically created by large surface lots. A hierarchy of streets can easily allow for a pedestrian-friendly side of the office development and a back service and parking side.

Other examples of important uses mistakenly isolated from centers are many cultural, religious, and civic facilities. The ubiquitous suburban civic center or entertainment zone is a lost opportunity to complete and reinforce town and village centers. Civic buildings, houses of worship, and cultural facilities can be integrated into the fabric of our communities, mixed with employment, shopping, and some housing. The modern equivalent of the courthouse square can be a focal point of our new main streets. Theater districts and movie complexes should also be an essential part of the centers that draw our communities together.

Light industry and factories, on the other hand, should be segregated. The low intensity of jobs in these areas, the need for frequent truck access, and the scale of the buildings do not lend themselves to mixed-use areas. Warehouse facilities and businesses that use toxic materials also need separation into special districts. In a way, big box retailing is a kind of light industrial use. It is, in effect, a warehouse that sells merchandise directly. These uses are more appropriate in light industrial areas than in village or town centers, unless they take on a more urban form, as we are just beginning to see in some central city developments. But regardless of form, their economics are often destructive to the kind of local, small-scale retail businesses that support the urbanism and civic quality of most centers. They represent one of the most vexing quandaries of urbanism: while providing the affordability that so many households need, they are destructive to historic main streets, local shops, and local produce.

Some other uses, such as college or university campuses, become special districts because of their functional needs. Certainly, the edges of these institutions must be clear and identifiable, but the relation between such special districts and mixed-use centers is a rich opportunity. The "town and gown" tension adds interest and character to many cities and towns throughout the country.

Preserves

Preserves are perhaps the most complex and controversial building block of regional design: complex because they include so many very different landscapes, locations, and potential uses; controversial because the means of saving the land and the economic impacts are hotly debated. Beyond those lands now protected by federal or state law (wetlands, critical habitat, and so forth), identifying which landscapes are appropriate for preservation is a major component of a regional vision. Natural preserves at the edge of a region are almost universally desired, as are open space corridors within the region. But their delineation and preservation can be a political and economic challenge.

Sometimes natural features give clear definition to the region; the oceanfront and mountain ranges of Los Angeles or the waterfront and lakes of Seattle are good examples. Often, there are few definitive natural boundaries. Denver or Chicago, with their surrounding prairies, are examples of regions without easily discernible natural edges. In most regions, simply preserving crucial lands is not enough to contain sprawl. Preserving unbuildable areas—wetlands, riparian corridors, steep slopes, watersheds, forestlands, and endangered habitat—will rarely define a complete regional boundary. In all cases, a combination of open-land preservation, infrastructure planning, and land use controls is necessary to direct the location and types of growth.

There are two distinct types of regional preserves: community separators and regional boundaries. *Community separators* function to create open space breaks between individual communities within the region. They are a high priority for communities seeking to avoid the "wall to wall" quality of many suburbs. Lacking sufficient size for large-scale agriculture, community separators are often preserved for local farms, habitat, or recreation. They can be created by cluster development that dedicates open space in a coordinated way, by the creation of urban growth boundaries, or by the outright purchase of development rights from property owners. Being closest to contiguous development and infrastructure, community separators are an expensive form of open space when not legally constrained.

Preserving farmlands as *regional boundaries* is a different matter. The land values are not as high, and the need for preservation is justified by more than regional planning. Preservation is critical because high-quality farmland is threatened in many areas of the country. American Farmland Trust reported a loss of four hundred thousand acres per year of "prime farmland" between 1982 and 1992.[2] Prime farmland often coincides with development because our major metropolitan areas tend to be located in river valleys with their typically rich soils. In fact, counties with high pressures for urban growth currently produce more than half the total value of U.S. farm production. But the issue goes well beyond actual farmland developed to what is called the "zone of conflict" surrounding development, in which farming practices are compromised. According to the American Farmland Trust, if 1 million acres of farmland are lost to urbanization in California's fertile Central Valley, as much as 2.5 million acres will fall into this constrained zone at the edge of development.[3]

Many tax incentives are currently used to preserve key agriculture, forestlands, and habitat. For example, the Williamson Act in California reduces the property tax burden of ag-lands. As the Trust for Public Land has demonstrated, the sale of open space easements can be partly financed by tax benefits. But it is still an uphill fight to preserve greenbelts and contain sprawl. This is largely because the urban land values that become available to farmers and ranchers overwhelm the tax incentives for preservation. So growth must be guided carefully by intelligent placement of infrastructure or, no matter how controversial, ultimately by growth boundaries and regional plans that specify specific preferred growth areas. Piecemeal preservation can support but not replace comprehensive green plans.

Beyond the need to preserve our agricultural capacities is a larger impulse among the electorate to preserve the rural heritage close to their urban areas, regardless of soil classification or ecological value. Whether for scenic value or the growing sense that local, fresh produce is healthy and ecological, this impulse has translated into ballot initiatives throughout the country to finance open space acquisition and purchase development rights. A complete regional design must integrate protected habitat with significant farmland preservation and scenic corridors. The tools to do so are as varied as the types of land that need to be preserved. Along with regional community separators, natural and farmland preserves are a fundamental structuring element of the region.

Corridors

Although corridors come in many types and sizes, natural or human made, they always constitute flow. Waterways, traffic, freight, and habitat movements define the unique corridors of each region. Corridors become either the boundary of a community or one of its unifying bits of common ground—a Main Street or riverfront are simultaneously destinations and passageways. Corridors are the skeletal structure of regional form and its connections; they form the defining framework of its future.

Natural corridors can be defined by specific habitats, unique ecologies, or watersheds. In most cases, they are a combination of all three. The interconnected quality of natural corridors is essential to their viability and efficacy. The more disconnected the system, the less ecological value it has and therefore the less power it has in shaping the built environment. For this reason, a regional approach to open space is essential, and preserving corridors rather than isolated parcels is critical.

Each region has a watershed structure that is fundamental to its natural form. Every watershed is made up of catchment areas (mountains and hillsides), drainage areas (streams, lakes, and rivers), wetlands (deltas and marshlands), and shorelines (beaches and cliffs). There may be other natural corridors worth preserving in the region—such as specific habitats of endangered species, unique ecosystems, or scenic corridors—but these four basic watershed domains are critical and contain many of the other types. Although many elements of a watershed (wetlands, riparian habitat, and shorelines) are protected by federal regulation, the results of the regulations are often piecemeal, emerging only as individual properties are developed and often in a disconnected form. Continuity is more important than quantity in natural corridors.

Using the region's waterways as a primary corridor system not only is ecologically wise but enhances quality of life. The American River Parkway in Sacramento is a good example. This twenty-three-mile park not only preserves valuable wetlands, habitat, floodplain, and water quality but also forms a major recreational asset for the entire region. It has become a kind of regional commons that everyone identifies with and enjoys. In many areas, these waterways have been lost to private development, flood control projects, or channelization. Recapturing them is a massive challenge, as is preventing further loss. Reestablishing lost waterways is part of the ecological repair and recycling that each region needs to undertake as part of building its open space network.

A striking example of the intersection among habitat preservation, waterway protection, and regional land use patterns has been created by the recent placement of salmon on the endangered species list in the Pacific Northwest. The regional land use implications are immense. Not only do the waterways themselves have to be protected with significant buffers, but the water quality and water temperature must be controlled from increased stormwater runoff due to development throughout the watershed. Because of this, the quantity of impervious surfaces and the design of detention and water-quality treatment systems become central features of the region. These systems then become assets within neighborhoods, just as the larger watershed elements create invaluable open space elements within the region. Ecology and urban design become inseparable.

Ironically, utility corridors are perhaps as important in shaping a regional plan as are the open space corridors. Investments in water-delivery systems, sewers, drainage systems, freeways, and other utilities form the backbone of development. If these investments push outward into areas appropriate for natural or farmland preservation, no amount of zoning and regional regulation will stop inevitable development. Designing these systems to be efficient, compact, and responsive to the land use vision of the region is essential. The urban service boundary in the Twin Cities is a good example of using infrastructure planning as a powerful tool in regional design.

Utility corridors must be coordinated with land use policy in both directions: they must be expanded and upgraded in areas targeted for infill and redevelopment, and they must be constrained in areas targeted for preservation. This coordination can be accomplished only at the regional scale, inasmuch as local politics often serve local development interests. Just as with highways, the bias of the past forty years has been to subsidize infrastructure at the suburban fringe—and this has been a catalyst for sprawl.

Reusing and repairing old, underutilized, and decaying corridors, either natural or human made, is an imperative for any regional strategy that includes significant infill and redevelopment. The strip commercial corridors of our older suburbs offer a chance, through redevelopment, to transform those areas into mixed-use, walkable districts. In these areas, the roads need to be redesigned and enhanced for pedestrian, bike, and transit, and the infrastructure must be upgraded for higher densities and a mix of uses.

Perhaps the greatest opportunity for corridor reuse is our underutilized railroad rights-of-way. Old, abandoned tracks can be reused for new transit links that run through the heart of a region's historic core and older suburbs. These old rail lines are like our old main streets—ripe for rebirth and supportive of the type of development most needed.

Corridors are the superstructure of the building blocks of the region—its neighborhoods, centers, districts, and preserves. Their design can create healthy limits and appropriate opportunities for infill or, on the other hand, can support scattered growth and community disinvestment. They can form rational boundaries and connectors for human-scale communities or they can fuel the next generation of sprawl.

The Urban Footprint: A New Planning Tool

These design principles, place types, and regional building blocks provide a new way of thinking about community development and, effectively, a new system of planning. Putting these elements together into a self-reinforcing whole and implementing it across the country is the challenge of the next generation of designers and planners. The taxonomy of neighborhoods, centers, districts, preserves, and corridors just described will eventually replace the old land use language of single-use zones—neighborhoods replacing subdivisions, village centers replacing shopping centers, and town centers replacing office parks and malls. In so doing, mixed-use urban places will become legal again.

A starting point to bring about such change is a planning tool called the Urban Footprint developed for the Vision California project. It employs mixed-use place types rather than single-use zones in the land use maps that typically regulate our growth. At the same time that it quantifies the place types, it links them to their key environmental, economic, and social outcomes. Using the Urban Footprint in regional and city planning allows mixed-use zoning to become normative at the same time that it provides essential data on critical impacts. In addition, each place type includes a set of urban design standards that can be used to replace outdated zoning. It is design, analysis, and zoning control wrapped into one convenient tool.

To accomplish this, the Urban Footprint provides standards for all the elements needed to build a complete community plan. In addition to the typical density and use regulations of standard zoning, each place type defines the mix of uses needed to create essential urban synergies, a circulation system shaped to its intensity, appropriate urban design parameters for its buildings, and environmental systems that are tuned to its unique ecology. It combines standards for urban form, land use, circulation, and environment controls in ways that are missing in planning today.

Endemic to our design problems is that land use, built form, environmental regulation, street design, civil engineering, and landscape standards are isolated and controlled by independent public agencies, regulations, and approval processes. What's more, each profession—traffic, civil engineering, planning, landscape, and architecture—has its own codes, which rarely sync with one another or to the particular qualities of place.

For example, road design adheres to standards based largely on the desired speed and volume of vehicles rather than the type of community the roads are serving. When a highway comes into a town, it should change in character, design, and speed. Or, when an arterial comes into a village center, it should provide for bikes, pedestrians, and parking—that is, it should be adaptive. Likewise, environmental standards often ignore place and impose formulaic regulations. A good example is the stormwater detention standards that require the same large ponding areas in both suburban and city center locations. While large retention areas are appropriate in low-density areas, open space in urban areas is precious and must be multipurpose.

Perhaps most problematic are planning standards for building setbacks and parking. These are rarely adjusted to fit unique places, and as a result our urban centers end up with suburban standards for large parking lots and sidewalk-killing setbacks. To create coherent communities, all the design elements must be coordinated and calibrated for each place—for each Urban Footprint type.

Most troubling from traditional planning is the omission of urban design in our zoning codes. The design parameters of buildings have been dumbed down to strictly quantitative measures—setbacks, site coverage, and height limits—and the quality of our cities and towns has suffered as a result. For great urban places to emerge, a clearer sense of a building's interaction with public space, climate, and architectural history must be understood and directed. Duany Plater-Zyberk & Company and other members of the Congress for New Urbanism have developed a groundbreaking tool called the Transect to address this missing element in the planning methodologies. In this system (described in detail in the SmartCode), six transect zones span from nature to the city center. The six zones provide a comprehensive framework for the development of urban design, landscape, street, and public space standards. Transect zones include Natural, Rural, Sub-Urban, General Urban, Urban Center, and Urban Core.[4]

The place types of the Urban Footprint model can be combined with the Transect to create a rich planning lexicon. The twenty-seven place types of the Footprint model provide enough variety and detail to plan a town, county, or city but can also be used to sketch out development at the regional scale. The place types are variations on the neighborhoods, centers, districts, preserves, and corridors described earlier. Each of the Urban Footprint types is assigned an appropriate Transect zone combined with standards for land use mixes, circulation systems, and environmental controls. As a result, the Urban Footprint model provides a way for cities to zone mixed-use areas that are comprehensive. A city or regional map using this system creates a complete land use and urban design code as well as an analysis that measures most of its significant infrastructure and environmental impacts.

The model can estimate a large range of collateral impacts beyond travel and carbon. For example, the individual buildings that make up a place type, when combined with its climate zone, provide the overall residential and commercial energy demands for that community. The same is true for land consumption, water use, infrastructure costs, and other key factors. As this process is almost instant, it means that sketch plans, alternatives, and scenarios can be examined with ease. In addition, the place types can provide the basis for a legal code that can be used by cities to control development.

The kind of transformation that the climate change challenge presents will involve more than analysis, consensus building, and vision—it will require a new set of tools, methods, and standards for the design professions. This chapter has outlined the land use elements that can make up a sustainable future. The systemic change in land use policy envisioned here will require such tools as the Transect and the Urban Footprint to be broadly applied. These planning tools will then need to be complemented by a new approach to transportation investments and street design. Simply put, we need to provide regional transportation systems that enhance transit and develop streets that encourage the pedestrian once again. As the next chapter illustrates, even well-designed urban places can be stranded without the right connections.

At one time, development and transit were co-evolving partners in city building; the urban center and its streetcar suburbs defined a uniquely American form of metropolis.

Along with a new approach to land use, a new circulation

system is needed: one whose goal is access rather than mobility. For too long, traffic analysis and street design have reduced transportation to moving as many cars as fast as possible, rather than the broader goal of providing accessibility for people. Access includes optimizing many forms of transportation—walk, bike, transit, as well as auto—and reducing travel before movement. Just as conservation precedes alternative energy systems in buildings, reducing the need for vehicle trips must precede all alternative forms of travel. Mixed-use community design can reduce the need for trips at the same time that it reinforces transit and pedestrian access. But it requires a new planning approach and a new design pattern for our streets and regional circulation systems.

Bringing daily destinations closer to home is a fundamental aspect of urbanism, as is the need for more and better transit. But to assert that we must build transit rather than freeways is simplistic, just as calling for infill development to the exclusion of new growth is often unrealistic. Many forms of transportation are necessary for regions to be viable. This is not to say that transit and infill should be ancillary pursuits, but that they are not and never will be the whole story. We need a circulation system that accommodates all modes as efficiently and seamlessly as possible at the same time that it supports urbanism throughout a growing region.

"Mode split" is the traffic engineer's jargon for how a trip is handled—whether by foot, bike, transit, rail, or car. Average mode splits in the United States show an extreme imbalance; over 82 percent of all household trips are by car.[1] Europeans use cars on average 40 to 60 percent less than Americans do. Comparing European and American travel behavior reveals not just the magnitude of auto use in the United States but also the relationship between the alternate modes. In all European countries, walking and biking—surprisingly, not transit—are dominant. This is because it is easier and more interesting to walk in their urban environments— they are dense, mixed use, with pedestrian-friendly streets. And biking is easier and safer on extensive networks of on-street and bike path routes. All this means that using transit is also more convenient, because one can easily walk or bike to and from it. Although many bicycle commuters pedal all the way to work, the European train stations often have multistory bicycle parking garages, jammed with commuters' bikes.

This pattern is self-reinforcing—more walking and biking means safer streets lined with more interesting shops; more transit riders means more frequent service to more destinations. A comparison between Sweden and the United States is particularly revealing. With a higher per capita income and a much more challenging climate, Swedes have the means and motivation to drive more. And yet, 49 percent of all trips are made by walking or biking versus just 11 percent in the United States; also, transit share is 11 percent compared to only 3 percent in the United States.[2] In Sweden, urbanism trumps both income and climate.

The way we design roads and street networks is key to these differences. The standard suburban circulation system is a strict hierarchy, with cul-de-sacs and local streets leading to collectors, which then access arterials and freeways—the only through roads in the system. The arterial network is typically based on a grid spaced at about one-mile increments. The problem with this dendritic, treelike system is that all trips, local or regional, are forced onto the same collector and arterial streets; traffic is concentrated rather than dispersed, and extreme congestion, even in low-density environments, is the result. In addition, there are no convivial or safe routes for pedestrians or bicyclists; they too must use the arterials to get to most destinations. Ironically, the typical suburban street network does not move traffic very well even while it limits walking, biking, and transit. Congestion in suburbia is one of the embarrassing conundrums of sprawl: it is not easy to generate traffic jams in low-density development, but the United States has perfected the paradox.

One could not design a system more destructive to the pedestrian. Even where there are sidewalks, there are few close destinations and too many dead ends. All paths inevitably lead to an inhospitable hike along the ubiquitous arterial. While no expense is spared for the car, pedestrians typically lack the sidewalks, street trees, and buffer of parked cars that make walking safe and pleasant. Intersections are sized for fast auto turns rather than for short pedestrian crossings. In fact, many are too long to walk across in one phase of the light. Even neighborhood roads are oversized, encouraging auto speeds that are a danger to bicyclists, especially kids. Design for cars overrides the unique quality of place every time and simultaneously destroys the possibility of walking.

The central flaw in this autocentric system is the arterial road. Lacking multiple, distributed routes, all local trips are forced to turn onto and off the arterial, causing intersection overload. The arterial road is designed for speeds that it never delivers, mostly because of congestion and frequent, long stoplights. This is all made worse by the need for long, multiphase signals because of left turns. For example, a trip down two miles of an arterial may average twenty miles per hour when the signal delays are counted, but the street is still designed for forty-mile-per-hour speeds. This useless high-speed design makes the road inhospitable to pedestrians and bikers, without really delivering convenience for cars. This speed criteria eliminates on-street parking, resulting in more off-street parking lots and ubiquitous sound walls. As a result, pedestrian-friendly housing or main street shops cannot front onto the typical arterial. Also harmful is the fact that arterial design standards are immune to their environment. The standards for speed, dimension, and design do not vary by place—the design is the same whether in a rural, suburban, or even city environment.

In this system, the arterial network inevitably pushes the design of developments in perverse directions. It propagates retail centers located at its intersections and strip commercial lining its inhospitable but very visible edges—all fronted by massive parking lots. Overlaying this arterial grid in rings and radials is the regional freeway system. The intersection of the arterials and freeway naturally becomes fertile ground for malls, big box centers, and office parks. This land use/transportation system is rational, coherent, and true to itself, even if increasingly dysfunctional. Its land use matches its circulation system in a way that mixed-use alternatives, when dropped into such a network, cannot. A transit line may occasionally overlie this network, infilling TODs and revitalizing some historic towns and cities. But short of such exceptions, new development is forced to grow within a circulation network designed for sprawl rather than for pedestrians.

The Urban Network

The alternative to the system prescribed by the traffic engineer's manual needs to be more gridlike and, ironically, less treelike. As in many natural systems, redundancy in networks is positive, providing resilience and reserve capacity. Redundant parallel streets are good; they disperse traffic along multiple routes and allow local short trips to take place on local, narrow streets. These also allow pedestrians or bikers to get to local destinations safely.

In such an alternative, arterials need to be redesigned for multiple users—transit, bike, auto, and pedestrian. They need to be part of a street system that connects communities rather than dividing them—that uses through roads lined by housing or pedestrian-friendly retail rather than strip commercial or backyard fencing. The alternative to the arterial should provide a new system of avenues and boulevards that provides for heavy traffic without always bypassing historic commercial centers— a road network that reinforces access to these centers without cutting them off from local pedestrian movement. Finally, the new system must incorporate transit in a way that is affordable, appropriately placed, and integral to the system.

Such a system of roads and transit lines was developed for Chicago Metropolis 2020, a regional planning effort of the historic Commercial Club (the same group that sponsored the famous Daniel Burnham plan at the turn of the twentieth century). One part of its regional plan for growth proposed a new street design system called the "Urban Network." In this system, three new types of roads replaced the "one size fits all" arterial grid: transit boulevards, avenues, and connectors. Transit boulevards combine the capacity of a major arterial with the pedestrian orientation of local frontage roads and a dedicated transit way. Avenues are multilane streets designed to welcome neighborhood uses and pedestrians along their edges. Connectors are more frequent smaller roads that provide for local access within neighborhoods with a gridlike set of parallel routes.

The quality and purpose of these three new road types are fundamentally different from the suburban arterial. Rather than sound walls and speeding cars, each is fronted with neighborhood uses and active sidewalks. Each integrates walking, biking, transit, and auto uses into one multipurpose right-of-way. At the same time that they husband the pedestrian and transit, they actually work better for cars. This is because traffic is dispersed over a grid rather than collected and focused onto overloaded arterials.

Transit boulevards are at the heart of this new network. They are multifunctional streets designed to match the mixed-use urban development that they support. They have dedicated lanes for transit—whether bus rapid transit, streetcars, or light rail. Like a traditional Parisian boulevard, they have a central area for through traffic and transit, along with human-scale parallel lanes on each side to support local activities and pedestrians. Transit boulevards are places where cafés, small businesses, apartments, transit, parking, and through traffic all can mingle in a sympathetic and time-tested arrangement.

Avenues are smaller in scale than these boulevards, lacking dedicated transit lanes but maintaining the capacity to carry local buses. At intersections, they support local village centers. Between centers, avenues create a parkway setting lined by large-lot homes or apartment buildings as in the historic neighborhoods of many great American cities.

Finally, a system of connector streets forms a finer grid within neighborhoods to provide direct access to local village and town centers. These streets are more frequently placed than suburban collectors, are interconnected, and therefore reduce traffic volumes to a livable level by dispersing trips. A key asset of this road type is that it functions to relieve the boulevards and avenues of local trips.

Within this more pedestrian-friendly network of streets, various mixed-use centers can find logical locations. For example, larger town centers would locate at the intersection of two transit boulevards, providing a high level of transit service for their commercial and retail businesses. Village centers could be located where avenues intersect, providing direct access by foot, bus, car, or bike from surrounding neighborhoods.

A good example of a large-scale application of the urban network is the plan for the twenty-thousand-acre St. Andrews urban expansion area north of Perth, Australia. This plan for a projected population of 150,000 uses a hierarchy of neighborhoods, villages, and towns set into an urban network of boulevards, avenues, and connectors. An extensive open space system buffers the coast, preserving the gullies that drain to the ocean and creating a green trail system throughout the community. As with any circulation system, the spacing and configuration of the network here bend to environmental constraints, topography, and existing development. A light rail system is planned for the central transit boulevard that connects the area's two new town centers to downtown Perth. A grid of avenues crosses the transit boulevard and leads to village centers and surrounding neighborhoods.

One key detail of this design is the way the avenues and boulevards transform themselves when entering a center. Rather than bisecting the center with large multi-lane roads, the boulevard splits into small pairs of one-way streets, called "couplets," separated by a block of buildings or parks. As a result, no street in the center is wider than two travel lanes. Ironically, auto flow is actually enhanced by these couplets because left turns cause no delays between one-way streets. In contrast, the greatest congestion on a typical arterial is caused by the extra time allocated to left turns at major intersections. This may seem like a technical detail, but it is central to the viability of dense, walkable, and urban places. In fact, most existing urban centers employ one-way street couplets to maintain human scale while they accommodate and disperse major auto flows. It is a powerful example of how streets must change and accommodate their context.

A good example of a village center organized around a couplet is the San Elijo Town Center, located about forty miles north of San Diego. This site, originally planned around the intersection of two arterials, was redesigned to place a village green at the center of four one-way streets. In one quadrant, a grocery store anchors main street retail; in others, housing and civic buildings line the streets. Two main streets lead up to the green, which is surrounded on all sides by mixed-use buildings. In two of the quadrants, a school and a community park complete the center. As in Perth, the center has no street bigger than two lanes yet it handles the traffic of two arterials.

Splitting the arterials into one-way couplets allows an urban grid to organize the site and provide for a more pedestrian-scaled environment. The standard arterial configuration would have had one intersection with a 166-foot pedestrian crossing, while the redesign had pedestrian crossings of just 24 feet. Counterintuitively, the traffic engineers actually found that the auto travel time through the center was reduced in the couplet system compared to the traditional arterial—at the same time that pedestrian movement was enhanced.

In Merced, California, traffic engineers studied a comparison of the urban network with a standard suburban arterial grid in a large new-growth area. Over twelve square miles of new development were configured in two different ways: one with clustered mixed-use centers located on the urban network, the other a standard layout of arterials and sprawl. The traffic analysis showed that, without changing overall density or land use, the traffic on the arterials was cut in half in the urban network. At the same time, the number of trips on the network's more frequent connector streets was reduced when compared to the suburban collector streets. The alternative design, with fewer total lanes of roads overall, led to lower road construction costs, fewer delays throughout the area, and better pedestrian flow. Fewer lane-miles actually produced a better circulation system for both autos and pedestrians.

In sum, the urban network is a circulation system that puts transit and pedestrians first while actually reducing auto congestion. If married to mixed-use development patterns, it can provide a model of growth that shifts toward a green urban future.

The Future of Transit

Since the demolition of America's streetcars in the 1940s and 1950s, transit, particularly in the suburbs, has been more a safety net than a true alternative to the car. It is no secret that we collectively decided to shape our culture and development patterns around the car. As a result, the density and urban form of most of our communities cannot support frequent or convenient transit. Currently, transit is believed to be too expensive and ill suited to our contemporary, auto-oriented metropolis. Our suburban destinations are too dispersed, and our bus systems, running on congested arterials and highways, are too slow to be an attractive alternative to the auto. It has become a self-fulfilling prophecy; the more we shaped our communities around cars, the more we needed them and, increasingly, any alternative seemed inferior. Not surprisingly, overall transit ridership across the country today is much lower than it was in the 1960s.[3]

However, in places that have combined land use policy with transit expansion, such as Portland, San Diego, Chicago, San Francisco, New York, Washington, DC, and many others, transit ridership has increased.[4] In these places, transit is seen as essential to healthy regional growth and downtown revitalization. New light rail systems have not only provided choice for commuters but have increased land values consistently along their corridors. Many of our most productive urban centers are transit dependent—they could not function without the extensive transit systems put in place over the past century. In San Francisco, 49 percent of downtown commuters take transit; in Chicago, it is 61 percent; and in New York City, 76 percent. Even in smaller cities like Portland or Seattle, a dense city core coupled with transit connectivity has one in four people getting to work downtown by transit.[5]

Most traffic engineers now agree that we cannot build enough new freeways to significantly reduce congestion in most of our major metropolitan areas. Many areas lack the budgets or the available rights-of-way to add significant highway capacity. Even if we could afford massive road building and widening, the land use patterns that such roads propagate quickly induce more traffic. As former Maryland governor

Parris Glendening has said: "We cannot fool ourselves—or the public—any longer: we can no longer build our way out of our highway congestion problems. It is not an environmentally or financially feasible solution."[6]

In addition, citizen groups in many areas have emerged to oppose highway expansion. Their gut sense is that more capacity will only breed more sprawl and traffic, undermining air quality, access to open space, and the economic vitality of communities. Not believing a significant shift in travel behavior is possible, many now advocate limiting growth rather than expanding capacity. But such growth limits simply drive development farther into the regional hinterland, leaving behind exclusive suburban pockets of affluence or declining neighborhoods starved for investment and redevelopment—more economic segregation, more congestion, and more sprawl.

Changing land use patterns alone cannot solve this problem. Walkable neighborhoods without regional transit, though an improvement over auto-only subdivisions, are incomplete. Convenient suburban transit linking the polycentric regional forms evolving in most places today is essential to a healthy pattern of growth and redevelopment. But our contemporary transit systems have problems; the costs of new light rail systems are often too high for the demand in many corridors, commuter trains are too limited in service times and too disruptive to neighborhoods, and the operational expense of expanded bus systems can be prohibitive. This is the Gordian knot of our next generation of growth: how to co-evolve community form and transit in an affordable and convenient relationship. How can we make transportation investments that are cost effective, that support walkable neighborhoods, and that focus economic energy on the revitalization of existing communities?

Unlike road systems, transit should be conceived hierarchically: from walkable and bikeable streets supporting local bus and streetcar lines to trunk transit lines with dedicated rights-of-way. This hierarchy is essential to transit's success. Leave out any element and the system becomes inefficient and inconvenient, resulting in what we now have: transit systems that need more subsidies than necessary and cannot attract a growing ridership. Each element—walkable places, local feeders, and convenient trunk lines—is critical. Without walkable and bikeable destinations and origins, transit riders are stranded at each end of their trip. Without local and feeder bus routes, people beyond the walking distance of a station are forced to "park and ride" or, as is more likely, just use their cars. Without trunk lines with dedicated rights-of-way and frequent service, the travel time for a transit trip becomes uncompetitive.

In the suburbs, walkable neighborhoods are feasible and expanding. Local bus service or streetcars in urban areas are increasingly effective in the context of these walkable neighborhoods, and feeder bus routes gain efficiency when connected to trunk lines that offer convenient regional service. Although each piece depends on the others, walkable environments are the foundation and convenient trunk lines are the catalysts. It is important to build every link in the transit chain. At present, light rail and walkable communities are often the missing elements in this hierarchy of service.

To resolve the "chicken-or-egg" problem of transit investments and supportive development, corridor plans that link land use to new or expanded service are necessary. Both land development and transit need years for implementation, so coordinated long-range planning is essential. Once a transit investment is committed and land use policies are updated, the two can co-evolve over time, with the transit justifying the higher development values and densities and with the increased densities enhancing ridership. A virtuous cycle is triggered.

The benefits of such integrated systems have been the subject of much debate and study. The preponderance of evidence now demonstrates that land use/transit integration does increase transit ridership, can revitalize declining neighborhoods, and can reduce overall auto dependence and carbon emissions. Simply put: "Research shows residents living near stations are five to six times more likely to commute via transit than are other residents in a region."[7] Other detailed studies show that compact development that is walkable, mixed use, and transit served can reduce overall VMT by 25 to 40 percent.[8] The complex interaction of land use and travel behavior has resulted in many new tools to model outcomes, and the outcomes always affirm the positive relationships.

As for the catalytic quality of transit, the results depend on a range of complementary factors, including zoning, public investments in pedestrian enhancements, and the like. But when the effort is coordinated, the results are dramatic. The East- and Westside light rail lines in Portland have attracted over $2.4 billion in investment within walking distance of their stations.[9] In addition, Portland's new $73 million streetcar line through the immensely successful Pearl District has resulted in $2.3 billion in private investments.[10] In Arlington, Virginia, the county invested $100 million to pay for enhancing Metrorail's location, unlocking $8.8 billion in private investment.[11] Reconnecting America, a nonprofit research center focused on transit, concludes that every dollar of public investment in transit leverages $31 in private investment.[12] The results speak for themselves.

Futuristic systems such as monorails are often held up as the next generation of transit. But the future may lie in simply reinventing the streetcar or light rail trains of the past and shaping them to the modern metropolis. Urban form has always configured itself around transportation systems and innovations. From foot to horse through rail to car, our cities have scaled themselves as much to transportation technology as to culture. If we are rediscovering some of the timeless qualities of our older urban forms and updating them to contemporary situations, perhaps the same will be true of our transit systems. The next revolution in transit may not be high-tech; it may be old-fashioned rail updated to be environmentally clean, scaled to the modern metropolis, and styled to new sensibilities.

Transit is more than a transportation system; it also comes with an intrinsic land use logic. In places that have integrated land use and transit, it has become the successful armature for a new generation of more compact and walkable development: Transit-Oriented Development.

Transit-Oriented Development

At one time, development and transit were co-evolving partners in city building; the urban center and its streetcar suburbs defined a uniquely American form of metropolis. This form was at once focused on the city and decentralized around transit-rich suburban districts. It offered the best of both worlds. During the post–World War II decades, this balance was disrupted by the elimination of the streetcar systems along with the rise of sprawl and freeways. Now, a new balance is emerging between suburb and city using Transit-Oriented Development (TOD) as a catalyst.

Transit-Oriented Development is regional planning, city revitalization, suburban renewal, and walkable neighborhoods rolled into one. It is a cross-cutting approach to development that can do more than help diversify our transportation system; it also offers a new range of development patterns for households, businesses, towns, and cities.

TODs are never stand-alone. They must be conceived in the context of, at the very least, a corridor and a metropolitan region. They are an alternative that provides choice not only in transportation mode but, more fundamentally, in lifestyle. As we confront the regional issues of open space preservation, of congestion and air quality, of affordable housing and affordable lifestyles, and of mounting infrastructure costs, TOD and its complex web of transit modes will become a more and more important strategy for sustainable growth. Although the TOD movement is still in its adolescent phase, there is much to be learned from the successes and failures of the current body of work.

The original direction of TOD was limited—focused on light rail to the exclusion of other transit types. Now the modes have matured to include bus rapid transit, DMU (self-propelled light rail), express buses, streetcars, commuter trains, and heavy rail systems. There is no one best system—the systems, like the land use each generates, are diverse and interdependent. The range of development types implied by each overlapping system will add compounding richness to the urbanism that is emerging. And as the transit systems expand, the location and types of TODs will further diversify.

There are three primary TOD locations within the region: urban centers, first-ring suburbs, and new growth areas at the regional edge. Within this spectrum lies a range of development opportunities. The potential for inner-city revitalization as a result of investments in transit and TODs is becoming clear but can still be enhanced. We have seen a return of regional retail to urban centers in some western cities partly as a result of transit development. Horton Plaza in San Diego, Pioneer Place in Portland, and The Plaza in Sacramento are early manifestations from the 1970s and 1980s of the nexus between light rail and the return of regional retail to downtowns. Simultaneously, residential renewal, even in decayed urban areas, is another manifestation of a larger movement back to urban living on the spine of transit. The Uptown District in Dallas is a startling early example of such a transformation, as is the more recent Pearl District in Portland or the Gaslamp District in San Diego.

The capacity for TODs in inner-suburban renewal has been demonstrated but not yet exploited to its maximum potential. First-ring suburbs, with their often vacant industrial zones and moribund retail corridors, are perhaps the ripest areas for the benefits of transit. The land is readily available, and the needs are clear. In these areas, many underutilized rail lines coincide with brownfield industrial redevelopment sites, just as the old arterial and highway alignments coincide with decaying commercial corridors. Transit and TOD opportunities are often perfectly matched in these locations. First-ring suburbs can redevelop if regional investments in transit are targeted and if financing for pioneering projects is underwritten.

The final, and perhaps most challenging, area for TOD is the new growth areas on the periphery of expanding regions. These outer areas do not enjoy the natural benefits of the "location-efficient" sites offered in the city and inner suburb. The viability of density and mix is difficult as land values are low and potential transit service is often far in the future. These areas tend toward low-density suburbs that cannot support transit or mixed-use development. But it would be very shortsighted to create a new ring of auto-oriented development at the regional edge. Here, a strategy for phased land use and transit that can evolve over time is critical. Such phased planning should start by designating and reserving rights-of-way for transit, express bus, and commuter train service. These preserved easements could then be utilized when the surrounding development has matured to support the transit system. Planning standards should allow critical areas to develop in a way that is receptive to adding density and more uses over time. The design of single-use commercial centers near proposed transit should always anticipate infill and intensification so that over time the area can be transformed into TODs. Here, planning for phasing and land banking is key.

All of this opportunity will come to naught without long-term vision and hard-headed implementation. One problem is the lack of systemic leadership for comprehensive solutions. Individual cities and towns rarely coordinate with other jurisdictions, much less collaborate on complex new transit corridors and complementary land uses. If anything, existing city fiscal incentives pressure municipalities to compete for the most taxable development.

Unfortunately, our current regional institutions are tied to local governments politically and rarely advocate holistic solutions. Their required regional plans are typically little more than a collage of individual town plans rather than a comprehensive vision of the metropolis. Finally, financing is a barrier to mixed-use projects like TODs because banks are structured to fund isolated single-use developments and underwrite them based on past successes rather than future needs. Add to this the fact that many local planning, parking, and traffic standards prohibit pedestrian-friendly design, and you have a short list of the challenges facing TOD.

All of this is changing, however. A growing and important role for regional governance is emerging around the country. Many areas have concluded that a laissez-faire approach to growth that defaults to local governments just does not work. The original impetus behind increasing the role of regional governance varies dramatically. In Oregon, it was to preserve agriculture and forestlands; in Washington, it was more general environmental and habitat issues; in Utah, it was a combination of fiscal and community needs; and, most currently, in California it is driven by the goal of reducing carbon emissions. But in all these cases, more efficient regional plans based on new transit investments and TOD have emerged as a central implementation strategy. And, as such, the barriers to TOD are being systemically eliminated one at a time. Regional MPOs are becoming more autonomous, planning standards are being revised, underwriting standards for TODs are being updated, and bonds are being passed to invest in new transit lines.

Sonoma–Marin Corridor Study

A quintessential example of TOD corridor planning is provided by a land use/transportation study for Sonoma and Marin counties. Just north of San Francisco's Golden Gate Bridge, these two counties are suburban in nature but in combination maintain a good jobs/housing balance. Historically, the area developed along a single rail line and later along a single highway. The eight towns in the corridor each have historic rail stations at their centers, having grown primarily around the train and ferry that served the area before the construction of the Golden Gate Bridge. The fifty-four-mile corridor has low-density sprawl in most of its new areas, but there is a beautiful core of traditional urbanism at the center of each town. It is an interesting footnote that Marin's historic neighborhoods—walkable areas such as Mill Valley and Sausalito—command some of the area's highest real estate values in the region. These older "Transit-Oriented Developments" are now very popular in the marketplace.

Because of the area's history, Sonoma–Marin's urban form resembles a string of pearls, rather than the sprawl that typically develops around suburban beltways. Its one freeway, however, is very congested and will remain so. The area's linear form works better for transit than the freeway, because auto trips are concentrated north–south rather than dispersed in many directions. Even worse, there are few parallel routes to relieve the freeway. This means that short local trips are often forced onto the freeway, where they combine with longer through trips to produce chronic congestion.

The study looked at five alternative land use/transportation strategies. The base case provided for some highway improvements and modest investments in bus service but for no major new transit and no significant land use changes from the existing low-density patterns. The second alternative added a new HOV (high-occupancy vehicle) lane for the length of the freeway with increased bus service. It was the most expensive alternative, at $834 million (in 1995 dollars). The other three alternatives combined rail service with bus, some HOV, and varying land use scenarios including TOD.

The first of these integrated alternatives included minimal rail service with morning and evening commuter-based schedules, some HOV construction, and no land use changes. This option was the least expensive, at $276 million, but would have captured only 5,800 train riders per day. Adding TODs to this minimal service of trains (every half hour during mornings and evenings) surprisingly doubled the ridership to 11,250 and cost little more, at around $300 million. This doubling in transit use resulted from modest land use changes, involving only a 5 percent shift in total housing allocation in Marin and 6 percent in Sonoma. This option showed that supporting transit with development did not require a massive change in land use policy but that it did greatly enhance the effectiveness of the system. The final option studied the possibility of increasing the rail service frequency to fifteen-minute headways at peak and thirty-minute headways during midday, at night, and on weekends. The ridership doubled again to 24,250, and the capital cost increased to $430 million, still close to half of the HOV-only option.

The level of ridership in the third scenario is comparable to that of many new light rail systems in cities such as Portland, Salt Lake City, or Sacramento. The surprising difference, given the ridership numbers, is that the Sonoma–Marin system is a suburb-to-suburb system without a downtown destination to anchor it. Such high ridership numbers demonstrate that the old assumptions about transit—that it needs a major city destination and that its corridor must be continuously high in density—should be revisited. The remarkable conclusion is that suburban environments can support rail transit if aided by TODs, if the technology employed is affordable, and if the alternatives are congested.

Regardless of the alternative chosen, the freeway remained congested—even in the option that widened the freeway for its entire length. None of the options studied could free the freeway from congestion because of its tendency to attract local as well as longer trips. More freeway lanes would simply attract trips from slower local streets.

This is a hard and critical lesson: transit does not necessarily fix highway congestion. But nothing else can either, for the simple reason that if freeway capacity is available people will use it. Even with massive road building in quantities well beyond the budgets of most regions, congestion will recede only temporarily. New auto-oriented development and the reservoir of pent-up local traffic will quickly fill it. Transit is necessary to give people an alternative to congested highways, not as a means to eliminate auto congestion. The fundamental goal of our transportation policy must shift from free-moving cars to access and mobility.

The proposed Sonoma–Marin system, which is similar to a technology recently proposed for Pittsburgh, provided very affordable operations, especially when compared with express bus. The study showed that express bus operation and maintenance would cost about $6.80 per trip, whereas rail would be about $2.90. This difference is primarily because the rail allows a higher driver-to-passenger ratio (driver costs are typically as much as 70 percent of operation costs for a bus system). Additionally, trains use less energy and require less maintenance. And, the HOV lane construction necessary to make the bus a reasonable alternative to the automobile cost approximately $700 million more than the rail system.

Walk, bike, bus, and rail options were all critical to the Sonoma–Marin system, as was an integrated system. Too often the elements of a complete system are operated by separate agencies that not only fail to coordinate the timing of service but also compete for funding. Such fractured systems are just another manifestation of the lack of regional coordination and its resulting inefficiencies. Like land use, transit must be designed as an integrated system at a regional scale without artificial boundaries.

Much was learned from the options in the study, and this information was used to fashion the final proposal. The preferred system combined investments in each layer of the transportation system. New bikeways, expanded feeder bus service, the new train system, and critical HOV links were included in a ballot initiative for a new sales tax. In addition, money for open space acquisition and a program for zoning changes were included. However, California had passed a conservative initiative to limit new taxes by requiring a two thirds supermajority for any local tax increases. This proved to be too great a hurdle in Sonoma and Marin, despite four ballots. Finally, in November 2008, in the middle of a recession, more than two thirds of voters finally approved the new "Smart Train" system.

Integrated land use/transportation plans such as Sonoma–Marin's are still rare and need a supportive state and regional political framework to succeed. The lessons are clear, however. Land use policy can have a large effect on transit ridership and the cost-effectiveness of transit investments. Even suburb-to-suburb patterns of travel can support rail transit. And, most freeway congestion cannot be solved with more roads or with more transit. In the end, only walkable urban neighborhoods and districts can permanently solve the transportation and congestion conundrum. The goal is to provide more convenience, shorter travel times, healthier and cleaner modes, and more choices in types of transportation in our communities—not more asphalt.

The most significant opportunity to reduce carbon emissions in California, and in the nation, is transportation—which in turn depends on community design.

The California Experiment
Chapter 7

California's capital, Sacramento, is in many ways a classic small

American city. With a current population of 400,000 in a region of 1.3 million, it grew during the gold rush as a riverfront trading city and quickly became an economic focus of the great Central Valley. Its simple American grid of streets and small blocks grew from the river port into a series of classic urban neighborhoods surrounding the current state capitol. Since the 1950s, it experienced many ubiquitous urban challenges; eviscerated by massive suburban growth, it simultaneously experienced destructive bouts of urban renewal. Growth in the 1950s and 1960s drained residential population away from its core neighborhoods and employment centers, dislocating the market for its downtown retail. As was true in so many American cities, its inner-city neighborhoods fell into decay as families left, shops closed, and schools failed.

Unfortunately, the remedies were often worse than the problems. New freeways designed to connect city and suburb destroyed more neighborhoods and cut the city off from its riverfront. Its downtown retail area attempted to compete with suburban shopping malls by imitation, closing its main shopping street to cars, which actually rendered the district less lively, more inaccessible, and dangerous. Then, finally, when Ronald Reagan became governor, the state created an ambitious urban renewal master plan for forty square blocks in the heart of the city, the first Capital Area Plan. The plan proposed demolishing most of the area, a once-thriving mixed-use neighborhood with traditional housing and a fine-grained street network, and replacing it with large office complexes on superblocks. Thankfully, this plan was never fully completed, but many blocks were leveled, leaving behind empty parcels and parking lots.

Under the administration of Governor Jerry Brown in the mid-1970s, Sacramento underwent a transformation; it became, in a way, the country's first experiment in green urbanism. Light rail transit was added to the city center and connected to the suburbs. Infill housing, historic restoration, and mixed-use development began anew. All new buildings were required to be green and incorporated low-energy solar design. Recycling programs, biomass power sources, passive solar architecture, and historic building preservation all became the norm. The state embarked on a radical plan to build "state-of-the-art" energy-efficient state office buildings, passed laws subsidizing mixed-income housing for urban renewal, and developed the now famous Title 24 energy standards for all new buildings in the state. This single set of standards helped set the state on an energy conservation path that has resulted in the average California emitting half as much carbon as the rest of the country.

Bringing all these programs together was a revised Capital Area Plan developed in 1976. Reagan's previous superblock plan was superseded by an "urban village" plan developed by John Kricken of SOM under state architect Sim Van der Ryn. The new plan emphasized urban conservation, land use diversity, and a transit- and pedestrian-based circulation system. In this new plan, "conservation" meant more than simply saving a few worthy buildings or reducing energy consumption. It meant conserving the most essential qualities of the city: its complex mix of housing, local stores, and workplaces; its historic twenty-four-hour community; and the scale and diversity of the old Sacramento street grid.

To reestablish the neighborhood while satisfying the state requirements for more office space, the plan called for a mix of low-rise, high-density housing, the rehabilitation of historic buildings, and the construction of new energy-efficient office buildings. Adding new housing for all income levels, along with local restaurants and shops, provided an opportunity for workers to live near their jobs. The plan gave special attention to pedestrian amenities and solar access while planning for the new light rail system. Streets were designed for more than cars, and buildings were required to respond to climate as well as urban context. New standards requiring all new state buildings to use passive solar and climate-responsive design were combined with urban design standards for mixed-use neighborhoods. Finally, the plan called for new architecture to be compatible with the scale and identity of the area's historic buildings.

Urban Solar Housing

Within the Capital Area Plan, a one-block development of mixed-income housing called Sommerset Parkside was developed. It utilizes passive solar strategies while mixing commercial space with a broad range of affordable and market-rate housing. The old Sacramento pattern of large detached dwellings, midblock alleys, and commercial corners is reflected in its site plan. The project mixes a three-story apartment building, a townhouse mews, and a row of detached apartment buildings. These differing building types reinforce a sense of identity and community for the occupants while allowing a natural social zoning. For example, one- and two-bedroom units enter from the street, while the larger family units enjoy the private yards of the townhomes. A variety of landscaped areas, unified by a bosk of pear trees, provide for recreation, privacy, and cooling microclimate effects. All of this is accomplished with a density of fifty units per acre, more than ten times typical suburban density.

Rather than turning away from the street, the design attempts to reinforce sidewalk activities and identity. Housing entrances, balconies, corner stores, restaurants, and street-side sitting areas all contribute to the life, as well as the safety, of the street. It is small affirmations like these that bind neighborhoods and, ultimately, cities together.

The light rail line that links downtown Sacramento to its outlying areas has a station across the street from Sommerset. In response, retail shops and a sidewalk café face the station. Dwellings overlook the street, with balconies above the café. A bank occupies the corner. The urban design works intimately with the new transit system, providing activities and meeting places for travelers, as well as "eyes on the street" for surveillance and safety. In return, the light rail delivers customers for the stores, activity for spectators to watch from above and below, and an easy way to get around. The interaction between the two—public and private development—has transformed a street that had been merely an access to office parking lots into an urban community—and in a way one of the first postwar TODs.

Gentrification has become a persistent problem for much inner-city redevelopment. As proximity to work and the vitality of the city is rediscovered by the middle class, the unintended consequence of their migration back to the city has been to crowd out the poor. Projects such as Sommerset demonstrate that a broad economic range can mix not only in one neighborhood but also in one block. One third of the project is subsidized for low-income groups, one third is priced for first-time buyers, and one third is priced at the standard market rate.

Not only did the project provide for a range of incomes, but it was also designed for a range of lifestyles. The unit plans—from three-bedroom family townhouses to two-bedroom apartments designed for co-ownership to one-bedroom units for elderly or single people—accommodate a broad cross section of the population. This mix of different age groups, incomes, and household types is, in fact, the opposite of our current housing patterns: projects for the poor, subdivisions for middle-class families, golf course communities for the wealthy, retirement villages for the elderly, and condominiums for singles. Such mixed housing was once the norm in cities and contributed significantly to the healthy and egalitarian complexity of the urban fabric.

Sommerset Parkside also showed that solar design could be easily combined with urban densities. In Sacramento, the elements of passive solar design are shading, orientation, landscaping, natural ventilation, and a careful balance between glazing and thermal mass. In Sommerset Parkside, every unit is oriented to the south and spaced to allow winter solar access. Its passive solar features became simple decorations and amenities: canvas shades, balcony overhangs, night insulation curtains, and plaster on interior walls. A throwback to past construction techniques, one-inch plaster on all interior walls acts as a cost-effective thermal flywheel—storing solar heat or cool night air while providing better fire and acoustic separation.

There is no reason that similar passive solar design and conservation cannot be applied to all new dwellings constructed in the United States. Sunlight, good ventilation, adequate daylighting, sensitive landscaping, shading, and sufficient insulation do more than save energy; they improve the quality of our lives and health. Differing climates obviously demand different design strategies, but this reinforces the unique qualities of a place and people's connections to climate and nature.

Overall, Sommerset is an early demonstration of the integration of urbanism and green development. It is diverse in its uses and users, it is human scaled and fits with its historic neighborhood, and it conserves energy both by reinforcing transit and the pedestrian life of the street and by using passive solar design in all of its details. In 1978, it was a dramatic departure from the norm.

Energy-efficient Office Buildings

Across a small park from Sommerset Parkside are two very different approaches to office building design. On one block are state office buildings (OB) 8 and 9, identical high-rise buildings set back from the street by a sunken plaza. Their height casts winter shadows more than three blocks to the north, making housing in those areas undesirable and reinforcing the single-use urbanism implicit in their design. Though they are unusual in having exterior sunshades, their tinted glass eliminates the possibility of natural lighting and necessitates an interior bathed with fluorescent illumination. The buildings are symmetrical on all sides, ignoring the implications of the sun, views, or the qualities of the different streets around them. This indifference to place, sun, and climate results in annual energy loads much greater than the national average. The lobbies are grand but offer no place to linger, meet, or socialize. The plaza to the north of one of the buildings is cold and uncomfortable most of the winter, and, because the street trees were eliminated, too hot in the summer. From a distance, the buildings form a conspicuous monument looming above the tree canopy, but from the street, they present no sign of life and offer no shelter or public activity. Like too many modernist buildings, they ignore climate, neighborhood, and the qualitative needs of their occupants, favoring an abstract expression of uniformity.

In contrast, the state office building across the street, called the Bateson Building after renowned anthropologist Gregory Bateson, attempts to respond to a broader range of concerns. Designed as a model for the Brown administration's energy conservation policies, its plan is nearly the inverse of OB 8 and 9—it is built to the street edge and is four stories high with a grand solar courtyard in the center. The courtyard is warmed in the winter by the sun and cooled in summer by shades and with night ventilation. This courtyard has become a special place for workers and the public to meet, lunch, listen to speakers or performers, and generally socialize. Simultaneously, the courtyard acts as a thermal buffer for the building, reducing heat loss and heat gain through the walls while providing daylight to the interior.

The building is friendly to the pedestrian, offering small sheltered plazas located at two of its corners, care for the existing street trees, and a small landscaped buffer along the sidewalk. On the exterior, balconies provide shade, add life to the street, and give workers easy access to the outside at each level. A large dining balcony is located over the main entry overlooking the park. Each facade is different in response to its solar orientation: the south is shaded by deep trellises and decks, the east and west have colorful canvas shades that retract, and the north has simple clear glass to maximize daylight. This facade variation, along with the decks, wood siding, and landscaping, makes the building compatible with a mixed residential neighborhood.

Many of its climate-responsive systems result in a more varied and satisfying work environment. For example, the use of the exposed concrete structure to absorb and store Sacramento's cool night air in summertime eliminates the low-hung ceilings so ubiquitous in most office buildings. The building's clear glass and natural lighting are more interesting and, in some unquantifiable way, more humane than the homogeneous consistency of artificial light. Operable windows allow natural ventilation, personal control, and the immeasurable pleasure of actually feeling the wonderful breezes that grace Sacramento on summer evenings.

Shading, natural light, opening windows, and storing the summer's cool night air in the building's structure reduced the Bateson Building's energy consumption to one-sixth that of OB 8 and 9 while it created a more humane environment. Construction costs were no higher, but the life-cycle savings in utility, energy, and carbon emission costs were enormous. This is an example of how a green urban future can address climate change in ways that save money, create more humane environments, and support the vitality of urban places—the kind of win-win-win scenario on which the 12% Solution depends.

But the most stunning "green" strategy of the Bateson Building is invisible and unnoticed by most: it has no parking lot. Typically, an office building of this size, over a quarter million square feet, would be required to have more than one thousand parking stalls that would easily cover eight acres. Bateson sits on one Sacramento city block that is just two acres. Rather than surrounding itself with four city blocks of asphalt, the building depends on transit, pedestrians, and carpooling. The energy, GHG emission, and social implications of this simple shift are profound.

The Bateson's courtyard is a traditional urban building type. It is the natural consequence of buildings that follow the street and are shaped for natural lighting. The notion that courtyards serve an important social function was lost when cheap energy eliminated the need for windows to ventilate or light the interior of buildings. Without the simple hierarchy of public street, courtyard, and private room, our cities become anonymous, one place much like the next, with both the individual and the community losing their locus of identity. In many ways, climate-responsive design forces buildings to become more locally sensitive and socially responsible.

The use of daylight in commercial buildings also transforms their social and urban identity. The simplest daylit building is narrower from exterior wall to exterior wall, with higher interior ceilings and fewer partitions. This implies smaller working groups in more spacious environments with better views and facades that are more richly textured by shading devices. In almost every case, the environmental concerns reinforce the common spaces—creating places that too often are eliminated by the "building as machine" ethic.

It seems obvious that all buildings, and especially those where we spend eight or more hours a day working, should connect with their neighborhood, be energy efficient, and support a sense of community as well as privacy and concentration. The industrial vision was of buildings shaped for efficient production. Land development, like the economy, was seen almost as a factory manufacturing standardized products, be they for dwelling, work, recreation, or shopping. We now find that the resources to maintain such a single-minded view of existence are overwhelming—and that, even in succeeding, too much of life has been left out.

First-generation New Urbanism

Even though much of this work was completed in the late 1970s, Sacramento's Capital Area Plan, its light rail line, its climate-responsive office buildings, and its mixed-income housing are a perfect manifestation of the urbanism needed to confront the climate change challenge in today's cities. And much of it has stood the test of time; the light rail is expanding and is at the heart of Sacramento's new regional plan, the conservation standards were replicated statewide through aggressive new energy codes, and the urbanism has been expanded and maintained by the Capital Area Development Authority. Today, it is a thriving mixed-income and mixed-use central city neighborhood.

Ten years later, I had the opportunity to work on Laguna West, a three-thousand-housing-unit development to the south of Sacramento in the suburb of Elk Grove. This site had a preapproved plan for standard sprawl: large single-use zones, uniform lot sizes, wide streets with cul-de-sacs, no street trees, and few local destinations. The redesign became one of the first "New Urban" communities in the West. A town center complete with parks, community center, senior and multifamily housing, an employment area, and retail was placed at the center of the project. Radiating tree-lined boulevards connected to smaller neighborhoods with schools, narrow tree-lined streets, and a range of housing types. A light rail extension (that unfortunately was never realized) was to anchor the town center, and Apple Computer set up a major assembly and dispatch center.

The community that resulted is denser, more diverse, and more walkable than its surrounding developments—a first-generation manifestation, circa 1990, of what is now a typical alternative to sprawl. Its architecture was built from standard production homes but was more varied in size, cost, and type. The streets are not lined with garage doors, and alley-accessed homes with in-law units mix with more standard lots and multifamily housing. Townhomes and affordable small-lot houses were introduced into a suburban setting that had seen only single-family subdivisions and garden apartments. Its street trees are now grown, offering natural shading and comfort to pedestrians and birds. Kids walk to local parks, the community center, and schools, and some adults stroll to local shops and events. But without the light rail link, it fails to fully shift travel behavior in the ways that are most needed.

Shortly after Laguna West was planned, the County of Sacramento updated its general plan based on the then-novel idea of Transit-Oriented Development partly inspired by Laguna West. A set of design guidelines was developed to radically change the structure of suburban development from subdivisions and shopping centers related to arterials and freeways to a hierarchy of mixed-use places related to transit. At that time, the politically powerful Building Industry Association (BIA) thought such change would frustrate rather than enhance market needs and opposed the land use innovations. Some changes were made, but the BIA largely prevailed in maintaining the status quo.

Twenty years later, the Sacramento Area Council of Governments is leading the way with the state's most progressive regional plan built around the idea of TOD. In fact, their growth strategy reinforces the approach of Vision California. In the plan, they compare a Trend future of more sprawl to a more compact future of TOD and urban infill. In their infill scenario, close to 40 percent of future housing and jobs are located near transit. And densities are increased as single-family homes are scaled back from 66 percent in 2005 to 53 percent for the new growth increment to 2035. The results reveal dramatic differences. Foremost, land consumption drops by half, saving over three hundred square miles of open space and farmland. Auto dependence drops by a quarter, and carbon emissions just from the transportation sector alone are reduced 14 percent.

But perhaps the most dramatic difference is the political realignments. Today, the Building Industry Association supports the TOD plan largely because they understand that there has been a fundamental shift in the market demand for housing. Sacramento is now leading the state in planning for land use patterns that address climate change.

California's Climate Change Initiative

Since actions at the national and international levels to limit GHG emissions are faltering, local and statewide efforts become more important. Natural market forces can accomplish much by implementing simple conservation and cost-effective technologies—but urbanism will need land use support at the state and regional level to become an effective partner. The Rocky Mountain Institute is rich in anecdotes and analysis of the economic benefits of conservation and new technologies—especially if the price of energy goes up. Efficient buildings are becoming typical even without stringent new standards as payback periods get shorter for landlords and residents, and as LEED (Leadership in Energy and Environmental Design) ratings for green practices gain traction in the marketplace. In addition, high-MPG cars are clearly growing in popularity. But more systemic change in our land use patterns and energy infrastructure is the missing link. The political momentum for change lies with states and regions rather than with nations.

California is now pioneering the difficult task of configuring a comprehensive approach to taming carbon emissions, including land use policies. In 2006, the state passed AB 32, the California Global Warming Solutions Act. It set goals to push down carbon emissions to 1990 levels in 2020 and to 80 percent of 1990 levels by 2050. In order to accomplish these ambitious goals, California is addressing the four areas covered in the Vision California scenarios—buildings, transportation, electric generation, and urbanism—as well as new approaches for industry and agriculture (see chapter 8). Their first pass at constructing a set of policies and standards is still under way as of this writing, and answers to the critical question of "how much of each" of the many technologies, investments, and regulations are still being formulated. The Urban Footprint model is being used to simulate and quantify various scenarios to aid in the process. A review of just how the state's GHG reduction law is being implemented sheds light on the issues that must be resolved for effective action in other states.

California's approach is a patchwork that includes a dizzying array of options. In California, the average household emits 33 percent less carbon in total than the rest of the country.[1] That is partly because of progressive building energy standards adopted in the 1970s and partly because of a mild climate. This translates into dramatically reduced residential and commercial energy consumption—California's buildings emit less than half of the national GHG average on a per capita basis.[2] In addition, California's economy has proportionately less heavy industry and therefore emits dramatically less in that sector. Finally, its utilities have a greater percentage of renewable sources—currently hydro but also a growing solar and wind sector. Unfortunately, the average California household tallies a modest one sixth less fuel consumption and auto miles compared to the rest of the country.[3] While California has done a great job in reducing energy consumption in buildings and industry, its biggest challenge going forward is transportation.

The California Air Resources Board (CARB) is charged with establishing standards and policies to achieve the AB 32 goals. They are employing a range of strategies that have been covered in this book: cap-and-trade standards for industry and electric utilities, building energy standards, new auto fuel-efficiency standards, and land use policies to reduce auto use. Exactly how these various strategies will be phased and combined is the work at hand, and it is extremely political. The draft Scoping Plan developed by CARB in 2008 lays out a first-pass allocation of target reductions for each sector of the economy along with technologies and policies for implementation by the year 2020.[4]

Given the relatively short target date, their plan focuses on technical fixes and conservation. The single largest target reduction, at 27 percent of the 174 million metric ton reduction required by law, is accomplished through standards for increased auto efficiency mandated by legislation authored by California senator Fran Pavley (which became national standards eight years after becoming California standards). By 2020, Pavley would set new cars at an average of 36 miles per gallon (MPG), resulting in an overall fleet that would perform at about 22 MPG. Setting aggressive auto-efficiency standards has been a controversial program at the national level. Yet many understand that if our auto industry does not lead the way to higher-MPG vehicles, it will fall behind in the global market as well as miss an opportunity to help improve America's air quality, reduce foreign oil dependence, and reduce greenhouse gas emissions. In 2005, California applied to the EPA for a waiver seeking the right to implement the standards at the state level.[5] Under the Bush administration that request was denied, but it was finally approved under the Obama administration in 2009. It calls for a 22 percent reduction in new passenger vehicle emissions by 2012 and a 33 percent reduction by 2020.

The Scoping Plan also identifies a cap-and-trade program as one of its main strategies, providing around 20 percent of the target. This program will act as an umbrella over many individual strategies deployed by industry and utilities. California is working closely with six other western states and four Canadian provinces through the Western Climate Initiative (WCI) to design a regional cap-and-trade program that can deliver GHG emission reductions at costs lower than could be realized through a California-only program. By California law, CARB must adopt cap-and-trade regulations by 2011, with the program beginning in 2012. Many see these efforts as a model for the national policies to address climate change.

Another significant state initiative involves a constellation of energy-efficiency strategies that include standards for buildings, appliances, and on-site power generation. This combination provides around 15 percent of the required reductions. The state's Green Building program is at the heart of this initiative and combines a range of implementation strategies. The Zero Net Energy program looks to reduce energy consumption in new buildings to zero through demand reductions, intelligent passive solar design, photovoltaic electric systems, and community-scaled cogeneration systems powered by green energy sources. These new techniques, along with improved construction regulations for new buildings, lighting energy reductions, and appliance efficiency standards, not only address carbon targets of the law but will also reduce the need for additional base-load electric generation.

But the existing building stock is a more intractable challenge. The Scoping Plan acknowledges: "In fact, improving the efficiency of California's existing building stocks is the single most important activity to reduced GHG emissions within the electricity and natural gas sectors."[6] Retrofit, weatherization, and rehab programs are central to solving this challenge, but the financial and regulatory hurdles are still ill defined.

Another major component of implementing AB 32 involves weaning electric utilities away from carbon-based fuels toward renewables. To strengthen and focus this effort, Governor Arnold Schwarzenegger directed CARB to establish a 33 percent renewable energy target for electric utilities by 2020. Currently, California's renewable electric supply is approximately 14 percent. Moving it to more solar, geothermal, wind, and small hydro will involve significant changes in technology, financing, and regulations.[7] A new distribution grid will be required to move power from renewable energy locations throughout the eleven states and provinces in the WCI to the various urban demand areas.

Unfortunately, environmental approvals to locate solar and wind systems are becoming a growing obstacle. For example, California just passed a law restricting the use of the Mohave Desert for a major solar thermal plant. Geothermal permitting is being delayed over concerns of triggering seismic activity, and new hydropower has a raft of habitat and endangered species problems. Added to this is the challenge of maintaining base-load capacity because many of the renewable sources provide only intermittent power. Energy storage systems become another technology that must be advanced.

All of these obstacles must ultimately be overcome, but the scale of deployment needed for each depends on the scale of demand. Reducing consumption through better buildings and more efficient land use patterns remains at the heart of feasibility for many of these renewable strategies. In addition, urban design is central to fixing the transportation sector, California's dominant and fastest-growing source of emissions. The hurdles to green urbanism are complex and varied but in all cases they can be solved with the right combination of political will, bureaucratic focus, economic investments, and professional commitment.

The Sustainable Communities Initiative

The most significant opportunity to reduce carbon emissions in California, and in the nation, is in the transportation sector—which in turn depends on land use. Analysis has shown that the carbon impacts of the transportation system cannot be mitigated by auto efficiency standards alone; the growth in VMT is too great to overcome. Assuming standard development practices in California, total auto use would increase by 70 percent by 2030. Even with standards calling for a 30 percent improvement in mileage for new cars and a 10 percent reduction in the carbon content of fuels, overall state goals would not be met. In fact, carbon emissions in the transportation sector would still be 10 percent higher than 2005 levels. The underlying auto-oriented land use patterns have to change.

Therefore, as a complement to AB 32, a new law, SB 375, was enacted in 2008 to require regional planning entities in California to create a Sustainable Communities Strategy (SCS) that reduces auto use and creates more integrated regional growth patterns. It is the first legislation in the nation to link transportation and land use to global warming. This truly landmark bill finally empowers the state's regional planning bodies to provide strategies that reduce GHG emissions while providing healthier and more efficient growth patterns: "Through the SB 375 process, regions will work to integrate development patterns and the transportation network in a way that achieves the reduction of greenhouse gas emissions while meeting housing needs and other regional planning objectives."[8] Moreover, alternative land use/transportation plans must be developed, giving the public and state choices it had rarely contemplated. Federal transportation and urban grant money is tied to these regional plans, so the SCS carries with it the incentive of major infrastructure funding.

The law requires proactive rather than reactive planning at the regional scale. Typical regional plans in California are little more than a compilation of local general plans. The sum of these parts often breeds sprawl as individual communities seek to limit housing and capture the lucrative tax base from commercial development. SB 375 empowers regions to correct these trends by providing a strategy that creates a jobs/housing balance and integrates land use with transportation investments in ways that will reduce auto dependence, congestion, and carbon emissions. In addition, the regional planning agency has to show how housing should be distributed within the region while respecting natural resource areas and farmlands. This process will begin to move California toward a green urban future in a way that new technologies and carbon taxes cannot.

As a key incentive for implementation at the local level, California's Sustainable Communities and Climate Protection Act allows local plans that comply with the SCS (along with other TODs and mixed-use projects) exemptions from state and federal regulations of greenhouse gas emissions. Now that the federal Environmental Protection Agency has designated greenhouse gases as a harmful air pollutant, they must be considered in all environmental impact reports and mitigations. But such impacts cannot be assessed at the local level—they can be effectively measured and mitigated only at the regional level. Any project, when seen in isolation, will increase local carbon emissions even if it serves to reduce them overall. For example, adding housing in a transit- and jobs-rich location will reduce overall auto use and emissions when compared to housing at the metropolitan fringe. But a local environmental impact report would not recognize this trade-off and would end up discouraging just the type of development most needed.

SB 375 recognizes this paradox and offers a way out: compliance with the regional SCS will exempt local projects from this new environmental constraint, and projects that do not comply will have to find other, more expensive mitigation strategies.

But key to this process is the carbon reduction target set by CARB for each of the MPOs across the state. If the target is too low, the legislation will not develop the true potential of urbanism in the fight against climate change. If set too high, implementation will prove difficult and a political backlash may overturn the whole effort. The state is currently taking on this challenge, and the effort itself is providing state-of-the-art thinking, innovative analysis, and new modeling tools. CARB is seeking input from experts across the country and from the MPOs themselves. The result will redefine the potential of land use and perhaps establish new directions for energy and cost-efficient development in general.

Vision California

One project that has grown out of these new challenges and legislation is Vision California (introduced in chapter 1). Cosponsored by the state's Strategic Growth Council and the California High Speed Rail Authority, this effort seeks to frame and measure various futures for the state comprehensively. It involves developing new analysis tools and using them to create a series of scenarios for future growth patterns in combination with a cluster of policy standards for conservation and renewable energy sources.

The new modeling tool differs radically from the current traffic analysis models in both ease of use and ability to accurately estimate the transportation consequences of complex, mixed-use, and transit-dependent developments. The old "gravity models," as the traffic engineers call them, were developed in the days in which autos so dominated travel patterns that their underlying assumptions lacked sensitivity to alternate modes and complex land use assumptions. They were effectively designed to size freeways and arterials, not to distinguish the complex impacts of urbanism.

The new tool created for Vision California, called the Urban Footprint model, is based on the design approach described in chapter 5. In it, land use is defined with a series of mixed-use place types rather than simplistic single-use zones. Vision California had used this tool to create statewide growth scenarios, provide a unified planning language, coordinate state investments, model the performance of the state's new high-speed rail proposal, and help with the implementation of AB 32. This unprecedented project will be the first time any state has created a unified model of its land use plans with the goal of optimizing its performance and investments.

Ultimately, political and economic factors will determine the final set of policies that will guide growth from the state's current population of 36 million to a projected 60 million in 2050.[9] How close California comes to the 12% Solution will no doubt set a standard for the country and for many advanced economies around the globe. An essential step to any progressive future is the kind of alternatives analysis that Vision California is providing.

The next chapter uses a simplified version of the Urban Footprint model to lay out possible land use/technology/transportation choices and consequences for the whole nation. It reveals major trends, significant factors, and essential policies that will be needed to shape a sustainable future for our country. Balancing the meta strategies of lifestyle change, conservation, and new energy sources can only take place based on data that reveal the complex synergies and trade-offs in what must be a whole systems design.

Like a cat chasing its tail, building alternate energy sources while allowing demand to increase exponentially is absurd.

Many groups have now developed low-carbon scenarios for

the planet built upon green technologies. Others have attempted to calculate the tipping points of greenhouse gases in the atmosphere and propose deploying large-scale "geo-engineering" to protect the planet. Common to most strategies is a goal of a maximum two-degree-Celsius temperature rise for this century—which, as calculated earlier, would require each person in the United States to reduce emissions to just 12 percent of their current rate by 2050.

To achieve this very ambitious goal, we will need a combination of smart land use policies as well as a broad range of new technologies, intelligent pricing, major public investments, and aggressive building standards. Understanding just how and in what proportion we combine such changes is critical to finding the right solution. Some promising technologies are autonomous; they can be applied to any land use pattern. Photovoltaic panels can go on any roof, and solar thermal power plants can be built in any open space blessed with good sunlight. Clean power generation through wind farms, geothermal, and biomass are all independent of urban form. Energy-efficient building design is somewhat independent, but the buildings in more compact urban forms have a head start. High-MPG cars can drive anywhere, as can electric cars.

So why not just leave it all to smart new technology? In fact, most approaches to solving climate change do just that—they are a checklist of green technology options. But such an approach will not lead us to the most cost effective, socially rewarding, or environmentally robust solution. If we can substantially reduce demand for travel and energy in buildings through urbanism before adding the new energy sources and technologies, the latter can be deployed in more modest dosages—ultimately, at less cost and less environmental impact. Like a cat chasing its tail, building alternate energy sources while allowing demand to increase exponentially is absurd.

Most green technologies have two principal outcomes: reducing carbon emissions and reducing reliance on foreign oil. As enumerated earlier, urbanism has additional benefits: lower infrastructure costs, less developed lands, more affordable housing, less travel time (meaning more time for family and friends), lower heating bills, lower auto costs, less water consumption, fewer parking lots, a healthier lifestyle—the list is long. While the focus here is carbon emissions and energy, these other benefits and cost savings will play a big role in a scenario's feasibility, desirability, economics, and politics.

In other words, getting to the 12% Solution will not be possible without a strategic mix. In order to understand what such a mix would look like, we have used a simplified version of the Urban Footprint model (described in chapter 5) to sketch out various scenarios for the United States that mix varying degrees of urbanism, new energy sources, and conservation. In scenario planning, the point is not to accurately predict the future but to bracket it and measure its inflection points—to understand what matters, along with the critical choices and their impacts. The goal is to study the outcomes of a range of futures and to plan proactively based on that information. Existing trends, emerging forces, new technologies, and long-range goals can be mixed when constructing scenarios. In this case, we posit a range of urban futures based on a mix of different "place types," or patterns of development, and then combine them with a range of green technologies and conservation policies.

Given that a combination of technologies and land use changes will be needed, what are the most logical combinations, where are the synergies, and what are the principal drivers that affect emissions? To model the choices and possible futures, we developed four scenarios by combining two land use futures with two alternative policy packages. While many alternates are possible, the resulting four combinations frame the issues well by setting out dramatically different but realistic options. The two land use futures are constructed by combining three place types in differing proportions: auto-oriented development, compact growth, and urban infill. The two technology alternatives are created out of the policies, new sources of energy, and conservation measures that affect buildings, autos, and utilities. These land use and policy alternatives are then combined into the four scenarios studied here.

The two policy alternatives combine varying degrees of new standards for auto efficiencies, building conservation, and utility energy mix. The three prime drivers of the policy alternatives are as follows:

1. *Auto technology*—measured by average MPG fleet efficiency and the carbon content of the fuel
2. *Building efficiency*—measured by the type of buildings, their energy consumption standards, their mechanical systems, and their climate zone
3. *Utility portfolio*—measured by the mix of sources (conventional, renewable, and nuclear) of electric generation and the efficiency of each system

The definitions and standards of the two policy alternatives used here, called "Trend" and "Aggressive," are independent of urban form. The Trend alternative is a simple extension of past policies and technologies. It assumes modest growth in vehicle MPG standards and low-carbon fuels, little improvement in building conservation design, and a stable mix of fuels in our power utilities. It is an alternative that results from little proactive policy at the federal or state level.

The standards used for the Aggressive alternative are derived from the options being considered by the State of California in its effort to implement AB 32, its landmark 2006 GHG reduction law. Each standard has a range of technologies that could contribute to its realization. For example, reductions in auto MPG could be achieved by hybrids, plug-in hybrids, full electric vehicles, biodiesel, or even hydrogen vehicles. Likewise, utilities could arrive at a green portfolio using a complex mix of renewable sources, such as solar, wind, geothermal, wave, or biomass. In these policies, it is not important to specify the exact mix and type of technology, just that the targets are feasible and can be a reasonable outcome of public policy, private investment, innovation, and new development standards.

Table 8.1 lays out the detailed assumptions of each alternative.

TABLE 8.1 POLICY ALTERNATIVES

	Trend	Aggressive
Auto Fleet MPG	25 MPG by 2050	55 MPG by 2050
Auto Low-Carbon Fuel	8% by 2050	30% by 2050
New Building Efficiency	10% improvement by 2020	70% improvement by 2020
Existing Building Retrofit Rate	0.1% per year	1% per year
Utilities	10% renewable by 2030	70% renewable by 2030

Two Land-use Alternatives

Before comparing the four scenarios, let me drill down a little into the types of communities represented by the two land use alternates, called simplistically "Standard Development" and "Smart Growth." In fact, each land use alternative comprises a mix of existing buildings and a large increment of new development—around 51 million new households by 2050, on top of the 117 million existing in the country today. Complementing this is about 10 billion square feet of new commercial buildings, in addition to the existing 74 billion. Depending on the scenario, existing buildings would be partially rehabbed or fully redeveloped at differing rates.

The "new development" component of each land use alternative is built by combining three place types: urban infill, compact growth, and auto-oriented suburbs. Each of these has a differing mix of housing types, a differing range of densities, and a set of design qualities that either support walking and transit or frustrate them. No scenario would be made from just one place type, and, depending on location, differing types would be more appropriate than others. So it is the mix of the three that determines the aggregate land use scenario. Table 8.2 describes the basic features of each place type.

TABLE 8.2 PLACE TYPE DESCRIPTIONS

	Auto Oriented	Compact Growth	Urban Infill
Single Family	82%	45%	10%
Attached Single Family	10%	30%	35%
Multifamily	8%	25%	55%
Transportation	Auto dominated	Walkable, local transit	Walkable, regional transit
Mix of Uses	Single-use zones	Mixed use, local destinations	Mixed use, regional destinations
Density	Low	Medium	High

The three place types used in the scenarios can best be understood through example. The redevelopment of the old Stapleton Airport in Denver is a good example of compact development. Its mixed-use plan has an average residential density three to four times that of the typical suburban development in the area. Although dominated by single-family homes, it achieves this density by mixing a large range of housing types, from apartments over shops and live/work lofts through townhomes and clustered bungalows. Interestingly, Stapleton commands a price premium when compared to typical subdivisions in the area, while it mixes income groups in ways once considered infeasible by the housing industry. In addition, its homes held more value in the 2008 downturn than their more standard competition. Part of this is because people like the scale, variety, and walkability of the community, and part of it is that the housing mix reflects a fundamental shift in lifestyles and household needs.

As a model of compact development, Stapleton demonstrates all the design principles described earlier as key to urbanism. It is *diverse* in its population and uses; a rich range of housing types are mixed with shops, job centers, parks, schools, and other civic uses. It is *walkable* and has *human scale*; its streets are designed for pedestrians and bikes as well as for cars, it is served by transit, and the buildings are shaped to reinforce the public spaces. It demonstrates *conservation* at many levels; the list includes reconstructing the streams and habitat destroyed by the previous airport, employing state-of-the-art building energy standards, providing water conservation and graywater recycling, and building a landscape with drought-tolerant and indigenous plants. Finally, it fits in as a seamless part of a *regional* vision that places new development in transit-served communities linked to the metropolitan center. Stapleton is just one of hundreds of such New Urbanist communities that have been built throughout the country since the early 1990s. Many in the development field now think that this type of compact master-planned community will come to dominate the housing market in the next decades.

The urban infill place type can take many forms and is inherently more sensitive to the surrounding context. In most cases it is denser than compact development and closer to metropolitan centers. Sometimes infill grows on small independent parcels that are redeveloped as a result of new zoning opportunities. For example, University Avenue in Berkeley has been redeveloping from single-story strip commercial to four-story residential mixed-use buildings in the fourteen years since the city created a new zoning for their gateway boulevard. In that time, hundreds of units have been constructed, and the level of crime, once the worst in the city, has been cut in half.

The Uptown project in the center of Oakland represents another type of urban infill at a larger scale. It was one of many projects that were the result of an aggressive city policy to reinvigorate the downtown by building close to 10,000 units of new housing, including 4,500 affordable units. The goal was to diversify the uses and the population of the city center. Rather than a downtown that was just a daytime employment destination, the new housing aims to create a twenty-four-hour community along with new local retail, restaurants, and major entertainment venues. Located over two Bay Area Rapid Transit stops, this revitalized city center is becoming an important regional location.

Examples of the auto-oriented place type can be found throughout the country in many forms and characters. Some very high-end communities attempt to be rural in their density and style. Others, designed for those of more modest means, are typically a series of subdivisions punctuated by shopping centers and office parks. In all cases, this place type is dominated by autos, isolates uses, has marginal transit service, and is low density.

The three place types used here are mixed in differing proportions to create the Smart Growth or Standard Development land use alternatives. Obviously, these are only two of the many land use mixes possible. Each region throughout the country could construct differing (and much more detailed) scenarios that mix a greater variety of place types in different ways. But this exercise is more of a sensitivity study that is meant to measure gross comparisons and bracket the range of differences. We assume the Smart Growth future would be made up of 35 percent urban infill, 55 percent compact growth, and only 10 percent auto-oriented development. By contrast, the Standard Development future would be made up of 70 percent auto-oriented development, 25 percent compact growth, and only 5 percent urban infill types.

One of the key outcomes of these scenarios is the overall mix of housing types that results. The Smart Growth option may seem a dramatic shift to those who believe the market for housing will remain focused on detached single-family homes. However, the change is not as radical as one might think. While it results in a significant shift in the *new* home types, when blended with the existing housing stock the final outcome is close to what many consider, given our changing demographics and economics, an appropriate range of housing opportunities. For new home construction over the next forty years, the ratio of multifamily increases slightly while single-family homes would drop from the current level of 62 percent to 33 percent. The difference is made up by a much larger percent of townhouse construction than experienced in the past. But when this new, more compact housing mix is blended with the existing housing stock, the result is still over 55 percent single-family detached. Multifamily remains steady at the current rate of 30 percent while townhomes move up to 14 percent of all housing—in the end, a good fit for the more frugal and aging population of future generations.

There are other differences between the Standard Development and Smart Growth land use patterns beyond housing density and type. While the Standard Development growth pattern leaves much of our current zoning and transportation investments in place, the Smart Growth alternative shifts toward mixed-use zoning that encourages walking for local trips and carries with it a major shift to transit facilities in transportation investments—fewer roads, more rails.

Four American Scenarios

Combining the two policy alternatives with the two land use patterns results in four scenarios. The combination of Trend policy and Standard Development is the "business as usual" future. In this case, land use continues in its low-density sprawling configurations, little is done to support new green technologies, and standards for cars and buildings are largely unchanged. Call this "Trend Sprawl."

The combination of Aggressive policies with Standard Development is an odd but significant future. In this case, we adopt a series of significant policies to support new green technologies and put in place high standards for building and auto efficiencies, but we do not change our current land use patterns or lifestyles. This scenario would be the result of some current thinking that seems intent on solving climate change without affecting our lifestyles significantly—new energy sources for old uses. Call it "Green Sprawl."

Combining the Trend policies with Smart Growth produces a simple measure of what land use alone can contribute to reducing carbon emissions along with all of its other co-benefits. Call this "Simple Urbanism." Finally, combining Smart Growth with Aggressive policies leads to the most potent outcome, one that involves the highest level of intervention in technology, standards, and lifestyle. Call it "Green Urbanism." The performance of these four scenarios is then measured on many levels. The following is a brief description of each scenario and its outcomes.

Trend Sprawl

This is a future created by extending current trends in land use and energy policy as if oil reserves somehow expanded to meet demand and climate change were resolved with some as yet unknown technology. We live much as we do now, enjoying the privacy of our yards and cul-de-sacs but spend more time in our cars. We still shop in malls and work in office parks. Our cities house a declining proportion of the population and jobs. Housing densities remain low and focused on single-family types, as has been the case for the past forty years. In 2050, the housing stock would be 67 percent single family, 10 percent townhomes, and 23 percent multifamily. This results in an expansion of our urban footprint by about thirty-five thousand square miles—equivalent to developing the entire state of Maine.

Such a footprint has many direct and indirect consequences. Open space and agricultural lands near our metropolitan centers are consumed at an accelerating rate—many regions double in size. The sheer magnitude of the area covered means that our infrastructure, roads, utilities, services, and regional water and sewer systems are all extended at great expense. The estimated cost of basic physical infrastructure is $47,000 per new house. In addition, public services such as fire, police, and schools are all stretched by the increasing radius of sprawl.

In addition, this low-density scenario results in high electric, water, and household costs. Because single-family buildings are typically larger and have more surface area, they are less efficient to heat and cool. The average single-family home needs over 105,000 gallons of water a year and 160 million Btu of energy. Because this scenario increases the percentage of single-family homes, the resulting average utility cost per home for energy and water would be $4,700 annually, compared to $2,300 today.

The largest indirect effect of this footprint is on auto use. The country would travel 4.7 trillion miles a year in cars (about 2 trillion more than today) consuming over 188 billion gallons of gas, largely imported. At $8 per gallon, this works out to almost $9,000 of gas a year for each household and about $12,500 per year for auto ownership, maintenance, and insurance. Driving combined with utilities would cost over $26,000 a year per household (in constant dollars), the current cost of sending a kid to many universities for a year.

Finally, the carbon emission of this future would be over 4.9 billion metric tons of greenhouse gases for the country, a 55 percent increase over our 1990 levels—rather than the 80 percent reduction goal needed to reduce climate change impacts. This level of emissions is split almost equally between transportation and buildings. This is a future that will need abundant new sources of oil, a very wealthy middle class, and a miracle cure for climate change.

Green Sprawl

This is the default prescription for solving the climate change challenge: new technology will save us without a change in our basic lifestyle or urban form. We will drive the same amount but in more efficient cars, we will live in subdivisions but with better insulation and solar collectors, and we will consume a lot of electricity but from renewable sources. And, all of these new technologies will generate a new economy, one based on clean energy. These technology changes have many positive outcomes that, while essential, are not sufficient to get to the 12% Solution.

Specifically, this future involves all the policies that lead to more efficient and green buildings, cars, and utilities. Buildings consume 70 percent less energy to provide the same comfort levels, the auto fleet averages 55 MPG and, in addition, is one third electric or biofuel based, and utilities have transitioned to 50 percent noncarbon fuels. It is a big step that is both necessary and possible. In fact, it is true that the strongest global economy will be the lowest-carbon economy, for it is a simple fact that by 2050 oil reserves will have peaked and their escalating cost will incur a tremendous economic penalty.

But this future has three problems. First, it doesn't achieve the goal of the 12% Solution. While it reduces GHG emissions to around 1.5 billion metric tons a year, that is still three times our goal for these sectors. Perhaps more technology could close this gap, but there is the second problem: the environmental footprint of the green technologies. Even with more efficient cars, we need a large land area to provide for renewable energy sources to power the projected 2 trillion additional miles of auto travel. We have already seen the unintended consequences of biofuels on food and water systems. A green utility system able to handle the additional loads for electric vehicles would need 1.4 million acres of high-efficiency photovoltaic solar farms, or over 9 million acres of wind farms, to support this level of electric car demand. Maybe nuclear energy will solve this dilemma, but it has its own problems in waste disposal. Because a unit of energy saved is much cheaper than a unit produced, reducing energy demands by reducing VMT always makes sense, especially when the conservation strategies have co-benefits such as better health and less asphalt.

Perhaps more significant is the sheer quantity of road and parking infrastructure needed to support these more efficient vehicles. This future almost doubles the total annual miles driven in the United States and therefore would involve massive new freeways throughout our metropolitan areas. Unlike the first generation of freeway construction in the 1950s and 1960s, these would necessarily carve through existing communities as well as greenfields and farmlands. The costs and environmental barriers would be extraordinary. The new freeway and highway capacity alone would cost upward of $4.5 trillion, or about $27,500 per household, by 2050.[1]

Finally, we have the third problem. Because this scenario does not change our land use patterns, we will have developed over thirty-five thousand square miles of new subdivisions, malls, and office parks. This additional land displaces farmland or habitat and will be costly to develop. The additional infrastructure burden to government and individual households will start at $2.8 trillion, or $47,000 per housing unit, for the basic infrastructure costs and will grow if the extended services are included.

Perhaps Americans in 2050 will be able to afford it, but the ultimate question is, will they want it? What will life be like in a green future of endless sprawl, congestion, and social isolation?

Simple Urbanism

Here, a change in land use patterns leads to a more urban future, but our technologies, buildings, cars, and power sources remain the same. This is not a likely possibility, but it gives a clear sense of the isolated impact that urbanism alone can have. The majority of new home buyers live in a compact community like Stapleton either in a small-lot home or a townhouse. They can walk to most local destinations, and their kids are safe to ride bikes to school and to friends' houses. More often than not, people use transit to get to work, and our cities have been revitalized with infill housing, thriving job centers, and new transit systems. Over the next forty years, we build 35 percent of future housing as urban infill and 55 percent in compact forms like Stapleton, with only the remaining 10 percent as typical sprawl. The resulting housing mix is surprising; when the new construction is combined with our existing housing stock, over half is still single family and multifamily remains about the same at one third.

This scenario's shift to townhomes and new multifamily housing results in a national urban footprint of just 9,300 square miles, only one fourth of the Trend Sprawl scenario. This compact footprint reverses many of the land use impacts of the Trend; less land consumed means more farmlands preserved, less infrastructure built, and less water consumed. The infrastructure cost per new house drops from $47,000 in the Trend to $23,000, and annual water consumption is down to around 87,000 gallons.

The greatest difference is in auto dependence. In this future, we travel just under 2.7 rather than 4.7 trillion miles per year and consume around 108 billion gallons of gas. This is not where we need to be, but it is a good start, in fact an essential one—VMT is cut by 43 percent. This scenario leads to savings in auto costs as well as home utility bills; the total annual cost is around $17,000 per home, almost a $9,000 savings per year over the Trend future. The annual GHG emission rate is close to 3,600 MMT, a 27 percent reduction without conservation standards or alternative energy investments—still not near our goal but heading in the right direction. Of these emission savings most is from transportation. The GHG problem remains significant because building energy standards are not upgraded, so while the more compact form saves considerable transportation energy, buildings are only 12 percent better.

Green Urbanism

So what are the implications for the nation if the Green Urban scenario becomes the norm? First, as with Simple Urbanism, there would be a drastically reduced physical footprint—less land converted from farmlands, habitat, and open space to development. If the nation were to grow by 140 million people by the year 2050 at current average densities, the 55 million new homes and their commensurate commercial development would consume nearly thirty-five thousand square miles. The Green Urban scenario requires only nine thousand square miles saving more area than the entire state of Maryland. Surprisingly, the mix of housing in 2050 is not radically transformed; it is 56 percent single family instead of the 62 percent today, and the quantity of multifamily stays the same, at about 30 percent. The difference in land consumption is largely the result of an increase in townhomes, small-lot single family homes, and denser commercial development.

The environmental implication of this reduction in physical footprint has many collateral effects. The quantity and therefore capital and operating costs of basic infrastructure (sewer lines, power connections, roads, and so forth) is proportional to land area developed. Less land consumed by the more compact communities means fewer miles of roads and utilities, less polluting runoff and soil pollution, less impervious surfaces to block aquifer charging, and less construction and maintenance cost passed on to cities and home buyers. These savings provide affordable housing through more affordable communities, with lower infrastructure cost as well as reduced travel and utility expenses. Growing with Stapleton-like densities as opposed to past trends would conservatively save $1.3 trillion nationwide in the cost of local infrastructure, such as roads, sewer and water systems, and other utilities— this equals about $24,000 per new household. Add operations and maintenance costs, which are borne by cash-strapped cities and counties, and the savings become even more dramatic.

More compact and efficient buildings mean less electric energy demand and fewer new power plants, for a national savings of over 4.3 million gigawatt-hours. A typical coal plant costs $220,000 per gigawatt in construction cost, and a wind farm costs $450,000.[2] So the incremental capital cost of not building the Green Urban future ranges from $245 billion if coal to $510 billion if wind. In addition, more compact, efficient housing saves in household utility costs. The average household would spend $1,800 on heating and cooling and $200 on water annually (in 2010 dollars), a savings of $2,800 when compared to the Trend future.

As one would expect, the Green Urban future generates a lower need for auto use. People can easily use transit to get to work, and they can walk or bike to local shops, schools, play areas, even friends' houses and open space. And when they do take the car, their typical destinations are closer and trips are shorter. In 2050, this more urban future provides an environment in which the average household has to travel only around 16,000 miles per year versus 28,000 in the Trend. Although dramatic, it is not unrealistic change, as many households in compact neighborhoods achieve that or lower auto use today.

If the next generation of development provided the walkability, transit connections, and proximities of more urban development, our national annual VMT would be reduced by more than 2.0 trillion miles per year. Think of the air quality implications, the reduced dependence on imported oil, the massive offset to carbon emissions, and the simple household savings in transportation costs.

In 2050, we would be consuming 139 billion fewer gallons of gas, producing 1,850 million fewer metric tons of carbon emissions, and spending over a trillion dollars less on gasoline—that's a savings of nearly $6,800 a year per household in gas alone if one assumes a gas cost of $8 per gallon in 2050. If one includes the savings of owning one less car and the reductions in house heating and cooling costs, the total annual savings would be nearly $15,000. Transferred to a mortgage at 5 percent, these savings would buy nearly $225,000 more home or education.

A final important implication of the reduced auto use is a dramatic reduction in health costs attributed to auto accidents, air quality, and obesity. The quantity of accidents is proportional to VMT, so one would expect about half the fatalities and injuries of the Trend future. To 2050, this could amount to a difference of over half a million lives, thirty million injuries,[3] and more than $2.5 trillion in accident-related costs.[4] Air quality health impacts are affected by emissions from mobile sources (cars and trucks) and single point sources (industry and utilities). Prorating the impact of halving the VMT on overall air quality and its health costs could result in upward of $1 trillion in savings.[5] Finally, obesity is partially related to a lack of exercise that would be mitigated in the Green Urban scenario that enables more walking and biking. Each hour spent in a car per day is associated with a 6 percent increase in the likelihood of obesity, while each half mile of walking lowers the odds by 5 percent.[6] With obesity-related diseases estimated to account for over 9 percent of total annual health care costs, just a 5 percent reduction in its incidence could result in more than $300 billion in savings by 2050.[7]

The truth is that these savings can be had today; just move from a large-lot home in a distant suburb to a well-insulated townhouse in a walkable neighborhood and sell a car. The problem, of course, is finding that townhouse and that kind of neighborhood. There, in a nutshell, lies the challenge of the next two generations of community development.

These savings are but one part of an overall strategy to create a sustainable future. Urbanism and conservation can provide over half of the GHG savings we need to achieve the 12% Solution. And, they can do it at a negative cost. The other half must come from industrial efficiencies, renewable energy sources, new agricultural practices, and carbon capture and sequestration. The political and economic hurdles for these are higher than for urbanism and conservation. The McKinsey study "Reducing U.S. Greenhouse Gas Emissions: How Much at What Cost?" shows that all the new clean energy technologies (except industrial efficiency) cost between $10 and $50 per ton of carbon abated. Considered broadly, it concludes that renewables would cost around $10 per ton, reformed agricultural practices around $20, carbon capture and

scenarios:
4 futures 2050

Trend Sprawl
The future looks like the past, with similar lifestyles and similar building and auto technologies.

STANDARD DEVELOPMENT   TREND POLICY

Simple Urbanism
Changing demographics and economics move us to a more urban lifestyle with more compact buildings and less auto use but technology remains carbon based.

SMART GROWTH   TREND POLICY

Green Sprawl
We still build largely low-density auto-oriented communities but with better technology; efficient cars, solar buildings, and renewable energy utilities.

STANDARD DEVELOPMENT   AGGRESSIVE POLICY

Green Urbanism
Here a more urban life is matched with efficient, clean energy sources, less driving in more efficient cars, better building technology, and green utilities.

SMART GROWTH   AGGRESSIVE POLICY

Each future is created by combining a land use scenario with a package of policies that direct auto, building, and utility efficiencies and energy sources. The land use scenarios are each a mix of development types that vary by level of urbanism. These four futures are meant to reveal the impacts of all these variables on a range of metrics, from carbon and energy to land consumption and household costs. None is a predicted future; they serve only to frame the issues and reveal levels of potential impacts.

PLATE 17

dialing in
growth

	Auto-Oriented	Compact Growth	Urban Infill
HOUSING MIX	**82%** SINGLE FAMILY **8%** MULTIFAMILY **10%** ATTACHED SINGLE FAMILY	**45%** SINGLE FAMILY **25%** MULTIFAMILY **30%** ATTACHED SINGLE FAMILY	**10%** SINGLE FAMILY **55%** MULTIFAMILY **35%** ATTACHED SINGLE FAMILY
TRANSPORTATION	**Auto** DOMINATED	**Walkable** & LOCAL TRANSIT	**Walkable** & REGIONAL TRANSIT
MIX OF USES	**Single** USE ZONES	**Mixed** WITH LOCAL DESTINATIONS	**Mixed** WITH REGIONAL DESTINATIONS
DENSITY	**Low**	**Medium**	**High**

Legend:
- auto-oriented
- compact growth
- urban infill

STANDARD DEVELOPMENT

5
25
70

SMART GROWTH

10
35
55

Land use scenarios called Standard Development and Smart Growth are created by combining three "place types" or typical development patterns. These three place types—auto-oriented, compact growth, and urban infill— each has a differing mix of housing types and densities along differing levels of mixed use and transit service. When combined they result in land use futures that accommodate differing lifestyles and incomes to varying degrees.

PLATE 18

dialing in
policy

	Trend	Aggressive
AUTO FLEET MPG	**25** MPG	**55** MPG
AUTO LOW-CARBON FUEL	**8%**	**30%**
NEW BUILDING EFFICIENCY	**10%** IMPROVEMENT	**70%** IMPROVEMENT
EXISTING BUILDING RETROFIT RATE	**0.1%** PER YEAR	**1.0%** PER YEAR
UTILITIES	**10%** RENEWABLE	**70%** RENEWABLE

These changes in building, auto, and utility performance are largely driven by public policy. The Trend policies reflect a future in which little new legislation or regulation is accomplished. The Aggressive policy set reflects some proposed actions at the federal and state level to set new standards for cars and buildings and through "cap and trade" begin to redirect utilities toward clean energy sources. All of these policies can be implemented without any change in land use.

TREND POLICY

AGGRESSIVE POLICY

PLATE 19

scenarios:
impacts

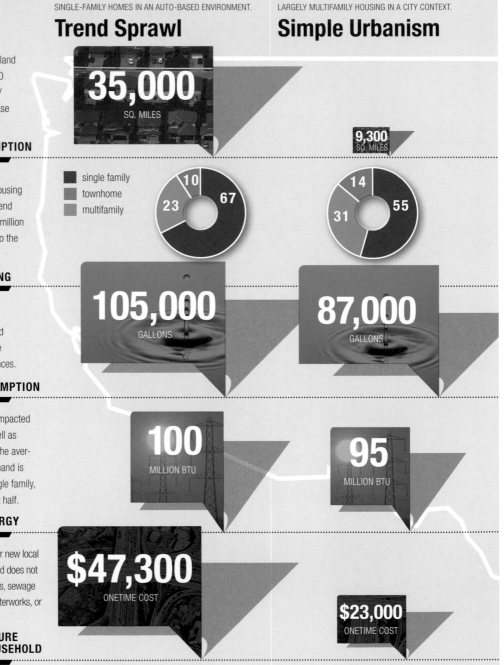

SINGLE-FAMILY HOMES IN AN AUTO-BASED ENVIRONMENT.

Trend Sprawl

LARGELY MULTIFAMILY HOUSING IN A CITY CONTEXT.

Simple Urbanism

The total urbanized land in the U.S. is 95,000 square miles. Trend/sprawl would increase it 38 percent.

LAND CONSUMPTION

35,000
SQ. MILES

9,300
SQ. MILES

The proportion of housing types shown is the end result of adding 60 million new housing units to the existing stock.

MIX OF HOUSING

- single family
- townhome
- multifamily

10 67 23

14 55 31

Water consumption per home is affected by yard size and the efficiency of appliances.

WATER CONSUMPTION

105,000
GALLONS

87,000
GALLONS

Building energy is impacted by home type as well as design standards. The average townhome demand is 75 percent of a single family, an apartment about half.

BUILDING ENERGY

100
MILLION BTU

95
MILLION BTU

Cost shown is just for new local roads and utilities and does not include new freeways, sewage treatment plants, waterworks, or power generators.

INFRASTRUCTURE COST PER HOUSEHOLD

$47,300
ONETIME COST

$23,000
ONETIME COST

PLATE 20

This set of impacts reflects a change in the built environment, either through land use or construction standards. The links are clear: as land consumption goes down so does the quantity and cost of infrastructure; buildings become more compact and energy wise; and water needs drop. The resulting mix of housing for the more urban future does not significantly change from current ratios, the country remains around one third multifamily, and the percentage of single-family homes drops from 62 percent to 55 percent with the difference largely in new townhomes. The Sprawl futures move toward a higher single-family ratio than today.

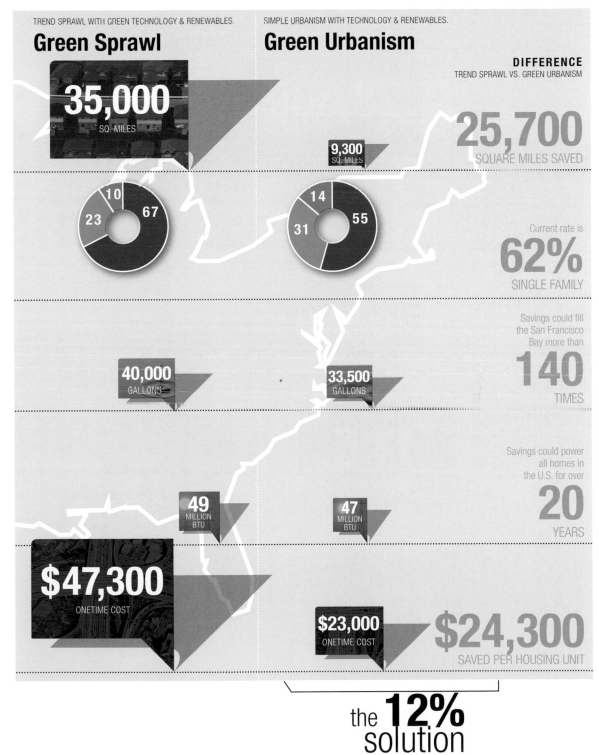

TREND SPRAWL WITH GREEN TECHNOLOGY & RENEWABLES.

Green Sprawl

35,000 SQ. MILES

10
23
67

40,000 GALLONS

49 MILLION BTU

$47,300 ONETIME COST

SIMPLE URBANISM WITH TECHNOLOGY & RENEWABLES.

Green Urbanism

9,300 SQ. MILES

14
31
55

33,500 GALLONS

47 MILLION BTU

$23,000 ONETIME COST

DIFFERENCE
TREND SPRAWL VS. GREEN URBANISM

25,700 SQUARE MILES SAVED

Current rate is
62% SINGLE FAMILY

Savings could fill the San Francisco Bay more than
140 TIMES

Savings could power all homes in the U.S. for over
20 YEARS

$24,300 SAVED PER HOUSING UNIT

the 12% solution

PLATE 21

scenarios:
impacts

Today the average household travels around 24,000 miles, in a Trend future that increases to over 28,000 while a more urban future reduces that number by 43 percent.

VMT PER HOUSEHOLD

Auto fuel consumption is a burden on our economy, the environment, and our security. Reductions can be gained through more efficient vehicles as well as less driving.

FUEL CONSUMPTION

GHG emissions summed here include residential and commercial buildings as well as personal transportation. These sectors represent over 50 percent of our total GHG emissions today.

GHG EMISSIONS

Over 15 percent of our urban areas now have levels of pollutants exceeding national standards. The resulting health costs and worker absenteeism are damaging in many ways.

AIR POLLUTION

Cost is the sum of household energy and water utilities combined with the expense of owning, maintaining, insuring, and fuel for transportation.

**ANNUAL COST
PER HOUSEHOLD**

SINGLE-FAMILY HOMES IN AN AUTO-BASED ENVIRONMENT.

Trend Sprawl

LARGELY MULTIFAMILY HOUSING IN A CITY CONTEXT.

Simple Urbanism

28,600
MILES / HOUSEHOLD

16,400
MILES / HOUSEHOLD

7.7
TRILLION GALLONS

5.7
TRILLION GALLONS

4,800
MMT

3,600
MMT

11.6
MILLION TONS

6.6
MILLION TONS

$26,600

$18,500

PLATE 22

Urbanism provides more places in which people can drive less. This results in lower fuel demands, less GHG emissions, less freeway construction, and lower air pollution levels. When combined with more efficient buildings this reduces average household costs for utilities and transportation significantly. It also results in less time in cars and the possibility of more time with family and friends.

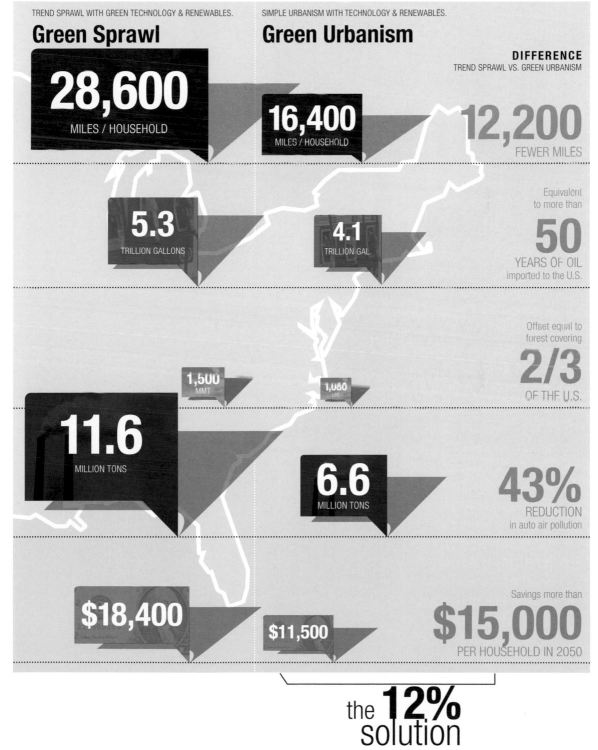

TREND SPRAWL WITH GREEN TECHNOLOGY & RENEWABLES.

Green Sprawl

SIMPLE URBANISM WITH TECHNOLOGY & RENEWABLES.

Green Urbanism

DIFFERENCE
TREND SPRAWL VS. GREEN URBANISM

28,600
MILES / HOUSEHOLD

16,400
MILES / HOUSEHOLD

12,200
FEWER MILES

5.3
TRILLION GALLONS

4.1
TRILLION GAL.

Equivalent
to more than
50
YEARS OF OIL
imported to the U.S.

Offset equal to
forest covering
2/3
OF THE U.S.

1,500
MMT

1,080
LBS

11.6
MILLION TONS

6.6
MILLION TONS

43%
REDUCTION
in auto air pollution

$18,400

$11,500

Savings more than
$15,000
PER HOUSEHOLD IN 2050

the **12%** solution

PLATE 23

As global population increases to what could reach 10 billion, with much of that growth in mega cities, a new vision of community and urbanism is long overdue. In fact, an urban form that is affordable, convivial, and environmentally benign is essential for human survival. If our cities, towns, and regions are to thrive, they will have to be designed for sustainability: systemically reducing resource waste and carbon emissions, balancing long-term consumption with sustainable production, and fostering social forms of integrity, equity and durability.

PLATE 24

storage around $30, and other innovations around $50. These four broad categories could save around 5.2 billion tons of carbon, the other half needed for 12% Solution. When combined with the savings of urbanism and conservation, McKinsey estimates the total cost at around 1 percent of the GNP—what is effectively a very low-cost insurance premium.

In sum, the good news is that a sustainable future is both possible and affordable. In terms of urbanism, the benefits extend well beyond carbon neutrality and actually save money and produce many co-benefits. In terms of emerging green technology, the change results in new jobs, new businesses, and global leadership in the next generation of energy sources. By any measure, this is not an onerous set of options to have.

At this critical juncture—when energy, environmental, fiscal, and national security challenges are converging—we cannot afford another generation of unsustainable growth.

A Sustainable Future

Chapter 9

I remember when President Jimmy Carter proposed sweaters

as an energy conservation strategy. He was right—dressing for climate and season has always been a natural and sensible part of life (and even fashion). But the idea that we had to compromise our thermostat settings and change our behavior, even in a minor way, resulted in political outrage. In the end, it seemed better to control OPEC even if it led to war—as it has repeatedly. Sadly, more than thirty years later, we still have the same three basic options: maintain our oil dependence through dollars and blood, implement a new set of technologies that can supply our current energy appetite with renewable sources, or build a more urban future and in so doing conserve more resources and change our lifestyle.

Blending the last two is really the only reasonable course. Defining the right mix and timing of the specific technologies, conservation strategies, and lifestyle changes is the current task. But urbanism, because it represents both a conservation strategy and a lifestyle change, is pivotal. Given this, there are two questions: How much land use change is possible? And, what impact would such changes have?

For many in the United States, the everyday lifestyle of freeways, subdivisions, malls, and office parks is a given—the inescapable underpinnings that structure our time, associations, and opportunities. It is all so familiar that this landscape seems immutable. It is assumed to be the inevitable consequence of market forces and steadfast cultural desires—a destiny in which public policy appears to play only a supporting role. It is unassailable because it is seen as the fundamental expression of an idealized and unchanging cultural destiny expressed through the free market.

The reality, of course, is that this form of growth is not just the inevitable product of free market forces; it is the product of a distinct, intentional planning paradigm and a highly coordinated set of policies and subsidies. State and federal highway standards and funding set the framework of its mobility; the secondary market and our tax structure underwrite its housing types, densities, and locations; and the financial needs of jurisdictions often direct its zoning. Over the past fifty years, a self-reinforcing system of federal, state, and local policies that promote sprawl has evolved. I will not enumerate here the many ways our built environment was subsidized (through federal highway investments, FHA standards, Veterans Administration loans, and deductible mortgages jump to mind) but will simply point out that such coordination is not really a conspiracy but an inevitable precondition in a complex, advanced society.

Unfortunately, this well-coordinated planning model is a form of growth that no longer fits our demographics, economic needs, or environmental challenges. We outgrew the "one size fits all" housing market some time ago. Much current market analysis supports the need for a fundamental shift to more compact, urban growth. In the coming decades, many aging owners of large-lot homes will want to trade to smaller, easier-to-maintain homes, leaving more and more McMansions on the market. At the same time, the market will have to accommodate a large number of first-time buyers seeking affordable housing and walkable lifestyles.

In short, the future market will trend naturally toward smaller homes, higher density communities, and more walkable and transit-oriented environments. New construction will shift from large-lot homes to bungalows on small lots, from plain vanilla detached houses to townhomes and live/work lofts. Condos will play a growing role for seniors and young singles looking for more urban environments, more affordability, and more flexibility. The net result will be a more urban future for America. After the housing bubble, we have the economic need, the market demand, and the environmental imperative to create a new direction in community development: one that will encourage, if not mandate, a new approach to planning, urbanism, and regional design.

Since the end of the Cold War, as the globalization of our economy has accelerated, the metropolitan region has become the basic building block of the new economic order. In today's global economy, it is regions, not nations, that vie for trade, tourism, and even economic dominance. In addition, our understanding of ecology has matured as we have come to realize that the region is also the basic unit in environmental terms. Because of the interconnected nature of ecosystems, social opportunities, and regional economies, we are now hooked together with our neighboring communities into a polycentric metropolis whether we like it or not.

As a result, we are beginning to set aside our outdated view of independent cities, towns, and suburbs and coming to see that the region is the cohesive economic and social unit. In the second half of the twentieth century, when the suburbs were affluent and older inner-city neighborhoods were declining, this relationship was not always obvious. But now, many older suburbs are in transition—indeed, some are in steep decline—and so it is impossible to ignore the fact that all our urban and suburban districts are interconnected. Old or young, rich or poor, the people of every metropolitan region are bound together in ways that greatly affect their daily lives.

The absence of powerful regional governance results in local development patterns that fail to consider the overall environmental and economic implications of piecemeal growth. The problem is multifaceted. First, local land use control is balkanized and unable to respond to such critical regional issues as jobs/housing distributions, transit, air quality, traffic, or open space preservation. Second, most local land use controls are outmoded as they are based on old single-use zoning. And third, federal policies and investments by habit redirect growth toward sprawl. As a result of these policy failures, we see a rising tide of building moratoriums as people attempt to deflect sprawl away from their communities. The result is a policy gridlock in which development is endlessly delayed, dispersed, and diluted—adding cost, but not quality, to growth.

Without a coherent regional planning strategy, the U.S. Congress, state legislatures, and local jurisdictions will continue to be limited to treating the symptoms rather than the root causes of our harmful development patterns. Foremost, we need a national urban policy that requires metropolitan planning organizations to develop regional plans that reduce auto dependence and GHG emissions through progressive land use policy and building standards. As noted, California has already adopted such legislation in SB 375, the Sustainable Communities and Climate Protection Act, which could serve as a model for the nation.

The justification for and implications of such a national policy are both reasonable and profound. It is clear that reducing auto dependence and its GHG emissions can be accomplished only through changes in land use coupled with increased investments in transit and pricing, signals that reflect the true cost of auto use. Any regional plan that demonstrates such shifts will not only reduce carbon emissions but also result in a long list of public benefits identified earlier, including improved health, land conservation, reduced infrastructure costs, reduced foreign oil dependence, and reduced water demands, to name just a few.

Such a policy would require each region to develop a set of alternate land use scenarios that quantifies investments and environmental outcomes. Each state would establish target VMT reductions for each of its regional planning organizations under guidelines set by the federal government. For example, the State of Washington has already passed legislation requiring a 50 percent reduction of total VMT from 2005 levels by 2050.[1] Once a plan to meet the target is adopted by the MPO and approved by the state, local governments would be charged with implementing the key land use policies of the plan.

Both carrots and sticks would bend local planning in this direction; noncompliance would result in reduced federal and state infrastructure dollars, while compliance would move jurisdictions forward in the funding stream. In addition, as carbon has now been designated an air pollutant by the EPA, jurisdictions that did not demonstrate compliance with regional policies would be vulnerable to lawsuits. Ultimately, each state would develop unique legislation to coordinate local land use control with the broader policies of the regional plans. Washington, California, and Oregon are but three examples of how legislation to coordinate local land use zoning with regional plans could be crafted.

In addition to the regional VMT reduction plans, many of our codes and standards would need to be updated. The federal government could take the lead, as it did in the 1950s, to develop new model codes based on best urban design practice. These could then be modified and adopted at the state level. Of critical concern would be updated building energy codes, land use codes (that include mixed-use and form-based standards), and traffic and road design standards that accommodate multiuse rights-of-way.

Unfortunately, the political adversaries of these integrated policies are large: localities looking for growth and tax base regardless of development quality or regional implications; developers looking for opportunities to repeat past successes without regard for changing times or new markets; neighborhood groups hoping to preserve and enhance property values by exclusionary practices; and people in general simply, and in some cases understandably, afraid of change or a loss of control. The forces for the status quo are powerful, self-reinforcing drivers. The defensive desire for a secure and exclusive private world and the tendency of specialists to follow rulebooks developed to solve past problems both conspire to inhibit change.

Such a major reordering of government policies and subsidies will require a powerful new political coalition. Fortunately, the multifaceted problems facing the U.S. metropolis can form the foundation for a powerful new alliance among environmentalists, developers, business leaders, and urban advocates.

Environmentalists increasingly recognize that a new form of development is necessary to enhance multiple ecological goals, of which climate change is but one. NRDC, the national Sierra Club, the American Farmland Trust, and many other environmental groups now actively support smart growth. Housing and jobs linked to transit are now as much a part of an environmental agenda as pollution controls or open space conservation.

Those urban advocates of inner-city investments and affordable housing now also support a regional approach. New transit systems and urban growth boundaries are part of their strategy to catalyze housing and commercial development in central city locations. By linking the two objectives, and by transcending the urban/suburban boundary, both environmentalists and urban reformers gain allies. Urban and affordable housing advocates all now understand the nexus between inner-city revitalization and regional planning for GHG emission reductions.

The private sector is also becoming an ally in these policies. The Silicon Valley Manufacturing Group in the San Francisco Bay Area is a good example. They understand that the long-term health of the region is key to their economic well-being and that an effective transportation system as well as a reasonable jobs/housing balance is at the heart of attracting and maintaining a robust workforce. Their advocacy of smart growth is reflected in the many enlightened business groups across the country, such as the Commercial Club in Chicago or the Bay Area Council in San Francisco, that understand that long-term investments and livability at the regional scale are essential to robust economic growth. Ironically, these business groups see more clearly the need for a regional approach than many local politicians.

Finally, real estate developers are moving toward smart growth policies. Regional plans that provide certainty and expedient entitlements would be a boon to the development industry. Current conditions force them into years of expensive, lengthy, and uncertain approval process. But ultimately, developers must respond to the marketplace, providing what the home buyer or business seeks. Mixed-use, walkable, and transit-served developments are gaining broad acceptance in a market that is growing wise to the shortcomings of stand-alone office parks, subdivisions, and shopping malls. The Urban Land Institute, the premier developer organization, has led as one of the most consistent and thoughtful advocates of smart growth with their research, publications, and community involvement activities.

These four constituencies—environmentalists, developers, the business community, and affordable housing and urban advocates—find common purpose in sustainable development in general. They can form a powerful coalition for large-scale ecological programs, expedited permit processing, efficient and affordable housing policies, and regional policies and investments that balance inner-city needs with suburban growth. In fact, new groups that include these formerly isolated groups are leading the charge for change. Envision Utah is a good example; led primarily by business interests, they incorporated local environmental groups, social equity advocates, developers, and church groups in their "big table" approach. In the end, the approach was successful because each participant shared a concern for the next generation—the developers because they would like to build for them; the environmentalists because they seek to preserve healthy ecosystems for them; the churches because they want to sustain a more stable community; the urbanists because they hope to pass on a more livable, equitable society; and the general public because they want their children and grandchildren to be able to live affordably and healthily in their community.

There is a special kind of wisdom in our cities born of the shifting forces of time. Each age brings with it a new set of priorities to which the city responds by constantly modifying and adjusting its form and character. For the environmentalist, the city is a mixed metaphor: on the one hand, a symbol of the congestion, pollution, and waste that modern culture has created; on the other, a compact alternative to the constant invasion of the natural landscape represented by modern sprawl. The old pattern of the city—with its mixed-use, lively pedestrian streets, public transit systems, and rich public spaces—had a human dimension that arose out of technical and environmental necessity. The form of many cities evolved before cheap gas and the auto's domination of the pedestrian, before electric lights replaced windows, subdivisions replaced neighborhoods, and malls replaced Main Street. Originally, cities demanded less of the environment in terms of land and energy simply because accessible land and energy were expensive.

While we cannot sustain the crisis of place represented by our current patterns of development, we cannot return wholesale to the form and scale of the pre–World War II American town. We cannot simply return to a time in which all people walked, the shopkeepers lived upstairs, and the neighbors were all on a first-name basis. For one thing, the auto, modern suburbia's godfather, will not disappear even if constrained and balanced by land use and transit alternatives. The extended family and the mom-and-pop shops will not return regardless of policy, design controls, or clever planning. And, unfortunately, the rich craftsman-like architecture built in small increments is largely a thing of the past.

But more finely integrated, walkable communities with a strong local identity and convivial public places are possible. The forms of these urban places will and should vary in time and place, but certain design principles will emerge as both timeless and contemporary—timeless in the sense that basic human needs and human scale do not change with the advent of each new technology, and contemporary in that certain traditions express fundamental characteristics of place and culture that are worthy of preservation.

At this critical juncture—when energy, environmental, fiscal, and national security challenges are converging—we cannot afford another generation of unsustainable growth. Instead, we need to build a foundation for a new version of the American Dream, for an urban pattern that is more accessible to our diverse population: single people, the working poor, the elderly, and the hard-pressed middle-class families who no longer need or can afford the Ozzie and Harriet version of the good life.

As global population increases to what could reach 10 billion, with much of that growth in mega cities, a new vision of community and urbanism is long overdue. In fact, an urban form that is affordable, convivial, and environmentally benign is essential for human survival. If our cities, towns, and regions are to thrive, they will have to be designed for sustainability: systemically reducing resource waste and carbon emissions, balancing long-term consumption with sustainable production, and fostering social forms of integrity, equity, and durability.

For the planet to thrive, the old patterns of growth built on the industrial principles of centralization, specialization, and standardization will have to evolve into new forms—forms that will replace modern architecture's symbolic gestures and trendy styles with purposeful designs that honor a place's climate, ecology, and history, and urban design that will replace short-term market forces with long-term stability.

The shift in our economy and culture from an industrial to a postindustrial base over the past fifty years has often been described as a shift from a "mass" economy to an "information" economy. Now we must create an "ecological" economy. Many economists and environmentalists are writing about a "green" future, but its shape, narrative, and balance points are yet to emerge. In the realm of public policy, it plays out in isolated policies, such as supporting renewable energy sources, greening industry, improving the efficiency of utilities, and adopting new conservation standards for buildings and transportation. In our private lives, it begins with growing awareness and small changes: recycling, changing lightbulbs, watching the thermostat, even investing in more insulation or solar collectors. But, as yet, it has failed to expand to fundamental change in our lifestyle or communities.

Urbanism is the foundation of that fundamental change. Urbanism offers the most cost effective form of conservation because it is better than free—it costs less to build compact, walkable communities than to build its alternates. And, these economies are only enhanced by all the other benefits it brings. Urbanism is a strategy to massively reduce carbon emissions and a way to preserve farmland and habitat, to enhance public health, to reduce infrastructure costs, and to control housing prices. At the same time, it offers the opportunity to rebuild our sense of community as well as enhance our national identity and resolve.

Design for a sustainable future will inevitably (I should say gladly) involve the integration of seemingly opposing forces: auto and pedestrian, large corporations and small business, suburban privacy and urban vitality, construction and preservation, private wealth and common well-being. These are poles that must be fused in a new pattern of growth. The resulting design imperatives are complex and challenging: to develop a land use strategy that radically reduces carbon emissions while it expands social equity and economic growth; to create communities that reinvigorate public life without sacrificing private identity and individuality; to advance a planning approach that reestablishes the pedestrian and respects our history; and to evolve a design philosophy that is capable of accommodating modern institutions and technology without sacrificing nature, human scale, and memorable places.

A big part of making cities and towns meaningful places rather than merely machines for shelter and commerce has to do with how we shape our commons. Ultimately, urbanism depends on the notion that the public domain must become richer as the private domain becomes more frugal—that success and well-being should be a shared, rather than a private, affair. It is this sense of the commons that makes places real, that turns "housing" into dwellings, "zones" into neighborhoods, "municipalities" into communities, and, finally, our natural environment into a home. Ralph Waldo Emerson, the great American philosopher and poet, translates this into an individual ethic that should apply to how we shape our communities: "to live content within small means; to seek elegance rather than luxury and refinement rather than fashion; to be worthy, not respectable, and wealthy, not rich; to listen to stars and birds, to babies and sages with open heart; in a word, to let the spiritual unbidden and unconscious grow up through the common."

notes

Introduction

1. Population Division of the Department of Economic and Social Affairs of the United Nations Secretariat, "World Population Prospects: The 2006 Revision and World Urbanization Prospects: The 2007 Revision," http://esa.un.org/unup (accessed May 5, 2010).

2. Kevin A. Baumert et al., "Navigating the Numbers: Greenhouse Gas Data and International Climate Policy" (Washington, DC: World Resources Institute, 2005), 32.

Chapter 1

1. U.S. Census Bureau Population Division, "2008 National Population Projections: Summary Table 1," U.S. Census Bureau, http://www.census.gov/population/www/projections/summarytables.html (accessed February 10, 2010).

2. U.S. Environmental Protection Agency (EPA), "Inventory of U.S. Greenhouse Gas Emissions and Sinks: 1990–2007" (Washington, DC: EPA, 2009), ES-17.

3. *The State of Metropolitan America*, Brookings Metropolitan Policy Program, http://www.brookings.edu/metro/stateofmetroamerica.aspx (accessed June 22, 2010).

4. Author's analysis of data from the World Resources Institute, "US GHG Emissions Flow Chart," http://cait.wri.org/figures.php?page=/US-FlowChart (accessed April 1, 2010).

5. Information about the assumptions, methodology, and results of the Vision California study and modeling tools can be found at http://www.visioncalifornia.org.

6. California Department of Finance, "Population Projections by Race," State of California, http://www.dof.ca.gov/research/demographic/reports/projections/p-3/ (accessed February 12, 2010).

7. Natural Resources Conservation Service, "National Resources Inventory 2003 Annual NRI," U.S. Department of Agriculture, http://www.nrcs.usda.gov/technical/NRI/ (accessed February 12, 2010).

8. San Francisco Bay estimate based on William Emerson Ritter and Charles Atwood Kofoid, eds., *University of California Publications in Zoology*, vol. 14 (Berkeley: University of California Press, 1918), 22; agricultural data from Economic Research Service, "Western Irrigated Agriculture," U.S. Department of Agriculture, http://www.ers.usda.gov/Data/WesternIrrigation/ (accessed April 1, 2010).

9. Research and Innovative Technology Administration, "Table 5-3: Highway Vehicle-Miles Traveled (VMT)," Bureau of Transportation Statistics, http://www.bts.gov/publications/state_transportation_statistics/state_transportation_statistics_2006/html/table_05_03.html (accessed February 12, 2010).

10. Bureau of Transportation Statistics, "National Transportation Statistics 2009" (Washington, DC: U.S. Department of Transportation, 2009), table 2-1. The fatality rate per mile traveled is assumed to hold consistent from 2009 until 2050. Hospital costs data from National Highway Traffic Safety Administration, "The Economic Impact of Motor Vehicle Crashes 2000" (Washington, DC: U.S. Department of Transportation, 2002), 60.

11. U.S. Environmental Protection Agency (EPA), "National Air Quality: Status and Trends through 2007" (Research Triangle Park, NC: EPA, 2008).

12. David R. Bassett Jr. et al., "Walking, Cycling, and Obesity Rates in Europe, North America, and Australia," *Journal of Physical Activity and Health* 5 (2008): 795–814.

13. U.S. Environmental Protection Agency (EPA), "Residential Construction Trends in America's Metropolitan Regions" (Washington, DC: EPA, 2010).

14. Christopher B. Leinberger, "The Next Slum?" *Atlantic*, March 2008.

15. Natural Resources Defense Council, "Reducing Foreclosures and Environmental Impacts through Location-efficient Neighborhood Design" (New York: Natural Resources Defense Council, 2010).

16. Andrea Sarzynski, Marilyn A. Brown, and Frank Southworth, "Shrinking the Carbon Footprint of Metropolitan America" (Washington, DC: Brookings Institution, 2008).

17. Author's analysis of data from World Resources Institute, "US GHG Emissions Flow Chart," http://cait.wri.org/figures.php?page=/US-FlowChart (accessed April 1, 2010).

18. Bureau of Transportation Statistics, "National Transportation Statistics 2009" (Washington, DC: U.S. Department of Transportation, 2009), table 1-32; Natural Resources Conservation Service, "National Resources Inventory 2003 Annual NRI," U.S. Department of Agriculture, http://www.nrcs.usda.gov/technical/NRI/ (accessed February 12, 2010).

19. Metro Regional Government, "1990–2008 Daily Vehicle Miles Traveled, Portland and the U.S. National Average," Metro Regional Government, http://library.oregonmetro.gov/files/1990-2008_dvmt_portland-us.pdf (accessed March 1, 2010).

20. The Center for Neighborhood Technology has done extensive research revealing that urban dwellers commute shorter distances and rely on public transit more often. Their per capita emissions, as well as spending on transportation, are consistently lower than those of the average American.

21. Office of Long-Term Planning and Sustainability, "Inventory of New York City Greenhouse Gas Emissions" (New York: Mayor's Office of Operations, 2007), 6.

22. Assuming advanced natural gas combined cycle plant technology.

23. National Energy Technology Laboratory, "Cost and Performance Baselines for Fossil Energy Plants" (Washington, DC: U.S. Department of Energy, 2007).

24. Calculations based on average capacity factors for each technology, and land use requirements based on case studies of representative electricity-generation facilities.

25. Energy Information Administration, "Annual Energy Review 2008" (Washington, DC: U.S. Department of Energy, 2009).

26. Al Gore, *Our Choice: A Plan to Solve the Climate Crisis* (Emmaus, PA: Rodale Books, 2009), 254.

27. Organisation for Economic Co-operation and Development (OECD), "Safety of Vulnerable Road Users" (Paris: OECD, 1998), 47.

28. OECD, "Safety of Vulnerable Road Users."

29. John Holtzclaw, Mary Jean Burer, and David B. Goldstein, "Location Efficiency as the Missing Piece of the Energy Puzzle: How Smart Growth Can Unlock Trillion Dollar Consumer Cost Savings" (Asilomar, CA: Natural Resources Defense Council and the Sierra Club, 2004); Front Seat, "Walk Score: Helping Homebuyers, Renters, and Real Estate Agents Find Houses and Apartments in Great Neighborhoods," http://www.walkscore.com/ (accessed February 10, 2010).

30. Prices per square foot are calculated using the online real estate services of Trulia.com using quarterly real estate statistics from 2009. Densities are calculated as a net of residential parcels using data from city and neighborhood boundaries established by the corresponding municipality.

31. Joe Cortright, "Walking the Walk: How Walkability Raises Home Values in U.S. Cities" (Chicago, IL: CEOs for Cities: 2009), table 8.

Chapter 2

1. Arthur C. Nelson, "Leadership in a New Era," *Journal of the American Planning Association* 72, no. 4 (2006): 393.

2. Nelson, "Leadership in a New Era," 394.

3. Author's analysis of data from the U.S. Census Bureau.

4. Bureau of Transportation Statistics, "National Transportation Statistics 2009" (Washington, DC: U.S. Department of Transportation, 2009), table 1-32; U.S. Census Bureau, "Census of Population: 1960" (Washington, DC: U.S. Department of Commerce, 1961), 1–146.

5. Steven Raphael and Michael A. Stoll, "Job Sprawl and the Suburbanization of Poverty" (Washington, DC: Brookings Institution, 2010).

6. U.S. Census Bureau, "American Families and Living Arrangements: 2003" (Washington, DC: U.S. Department of Commerce, 2010), tables HH-6 and FM-1.

7. U.S. Census Bureau, "American Families and Living Arrangements: 2003."

8. U.S. Bureau of Labor Statistics, "Handbook of Labor Statistics, Bulletin 2175" (Washington, DC: U.S. Bureau of Labor Statistics, 1983), 44; U.S. Bureau of Labor Statistics, "Current Population Survey (CPS)" (Washington, DC: U.S. Bureau of Labor Statistics, 2008), 195.

9. Robert Putnam, *Bowling Alone: The Collapse and Revival of American Community* (New York: Simon & Schuster, 2000), 27.

10. Putnam, *Bowling Alone*, 45.

11. U.S. Census Bureau, "American Families and Living Arrangements: 2003" (Washington, DC: U.S. Department of Commerce, 2004), figure 2.

12. U.S. Census Bureau, "Statistical Abstract of the United States: 2003" (Washington, DC: U.S. Census Bureau, 2003), no. HS-12: Households by Type and Size: 1900 to 2002.

13. U.S. Census Bureau, "2008 Characteristics of New Housing" (Washington, DC: U.S. Census Bureau, 2008), 384.

14. Federal Highway Administration, "Journey-to-work Trends in the United States and Its Major Metropolitan Areas 1960–1990" (Washington, DC: U.S. Department of Transportation, 1994), exhibit 1.14.

15. Federal Highway Administration, "Journey-to-work Trends in the United States," exhibit 1.1.

16. Federal Highway Administration, "Journey-to-work Trends in the United States," exhibit 1.1.

17. Federal Highway Administration, "Highway Statistics Summary to 1995" (Washington, DC: U.S. Department of Transportation, 1995), table VM-201; Bureau of Transportation Statistics, "National Transportation Statistics 2009" (Washington, DC: U.S. Department of Transportation, 2009), table 1-32.

18. Federal Highway Administration, "Highway Statistics Summary to 1995," table VM-201; Bureau of Transportation Statistics, "National Transportation Statistics 2009," table 1-32.

19. Federal Highway Administration, "Addendum to the 1997 Federal Highway Cost Allocation Study Final Report" (Washington, DC: U.S. Department of Transportation, 2000).

20. U.S. Environmental Protection Agency (EPA), "National Air Quality Status and Trends through 2007" (Washington, DC: EPA, 2008), 1.

21. Bureau of Transportation Statistics, "National Transportation Statistics 2009," table 2-17: Motor Vehicle Safety Data.

22. Bureau of Transportation Statistics, "National Transportation Statistics 2009," table 2-17: Motor Vehicle Safety Data.

23. Cambridge Systematics, "Crashes vs. Congestion: What's the Cost to Society?" (Washington, DC: American Automobile Association, 2008), 4-3.

24. William Lucy, "Mortality Risk Associated with Leaving Home: Recognizing the Relevance of the Built Environment," *American Journal of Public Health* 93 (2003): 9.

25. Gregory W. Heath et al., "The Effectiveness of Urban Design and Land Use and Transport Policies and Practices to Increase Physical Activity: A Systematic Review," *Journal of Physical Activity and Health* 3 (2006): S-56.

26. Pat S. Hu and Timothy R. Reuscher for the Federal Highway Administration, "Summary of Travel Trends: 2001 National Household Travel Survey" (Washington, DC: U.S. Department of Transportation, 2004), 17; Reid Ewing et al., *Growing Cooler: The Evidence of Urban Development and Climate Change* (Washington, DC: Urban Land Institute, 2008).

27. J. F. Sallis et al., "Neighborhood Built Environment and Income: Examining Multiple Health Outcomes" (Sacramento: California Department of Transportation, 2002), 1.

28. Laura K. Kahn et al., "Recommended Community Strategies and Measurements to Prevent Obesity in the United States" (Atlanta: Centers for Disease Control and Prevention, 2009).

29. U.S. Bureau of Labor Statistics, "Handbook of Labor Statistics, Bulletin 2175," 44; U.S. Bureau of Labor Statistics, "Current Population Survey (CPS)" (2008), 206. Basic industries defined as blue-collar workers and farm workers (1958); natural resources, construction, and maintenance occupations as well as production, transportation, and material moving occupations (2008).

30. U.S. Bureau of Labor Statistics, "Current Population Survey (CPS)" (2008), 206.

31. Energy Information Administration, "Annual Energy Review 2008" (Washington, DC: U.S. Department of Energy, 2009), table 2.1a.

32. Lawrence Mishel et al., *The State of Working America 2008/2009* (Ithaca, NY: Cornell University Press, 2009), table 1.1.

33. U.S. Bureau of Labor Statistics, "100 Years of U.S. Consumer Spending: Data for the Nation, New York City, and Boston" (Washington, DC: U.S. Department of Labor, 2006).

34. Richard Florida, "How the Crash Will Reshape America," *Atlantic*, March 2009.

35. Energy Information Administration, "Annual Energy Review 2008," table 2.1a.

36. U.S. Census Bureau, "Current Population Survey" (2009) and "Annual Social and Economic Supplements" (2009 and earlier), U.S. Census Bureau, http://www.census.gov/population/socdemo/hh-fam/hh1.xls (accessed April 5, 2010).

37. Bureau of Transportation Statistics, "National Transportation Statistics 2009," table 1-32.

38. Energy Information Administration, "Annual Energy Review 2008," table 2.1a.

39. Energy Information Administration, "Annual Energy Review 2008," table 2.1a.

40. Energy Information Administration, "Annual Energy Review 2008," figure 8.0.

41. Energy Information Administration, "Annual Energy Review 2008," table 2.1a.

42. Energy Information Administration, "Annual Energy Review 2008," table 2.1a.

43. Bureau of Transportation Statistics, "National Transportation Statistics 2009," table 1-37.

44. Center for Clean Air Policy (CCAP) and Center for Neighborhood Technology (CNT), "High Speed Rail and Greenhouse Gas Emissions in the U.S." (Washington, DC: CCAP and CNT, 2006), 10. The German Intercity-Express train was used for purpose of comparison. Its construction as electric multiple units most closely resembles the technology proposed for the California high-speed rail.

Chapter 3

1. Global Footprint Network, *The Ecological Footprint Atlas 2009* (Oakland, CA: Global Footprint Network, 2009).

2. Global Footprint Network, *The Ecological Footprint Atlas 2009*.

3. Global Footprint Network, *The Ecological Footprint Atlas 2009*.

4. International Energy Agency, CO_2 *Emissions from Fuel Combustion: Highlights* (Paris: Organisation for Economic Co-operation and Development, 2009), 89.

5. These figures take into account emissions from the full life cycle of transportation fuel use, which exceeds emissions from fuel combustion alone.

6. Author's analysis of data from (1) World Resources Institute, "US GHG Emissions Flow Chart," http://cait.wri.org/figures.php?page=/US-FlowChart (accessed April 1, 2010); (2) Kevin A. Baumert et al., "Navigating the Numbers: Greenhouse Gas Data and International Climate Policy" (Washington, DC: World Resources Institute, 2005), 4–5; (3) California Energy Commission, "Inventory of California Greenhouse Gas Emissions and Sinks: 1990 to 2004" (Sacramento: California Energy Commission, 2006).

7. U.S. Environmental Protection Agency (EPA), "Inventory of U.S. Greenhouse Gas Emissions and Sinks: 1990–2007" (Washington, DC: EPA, 2009), table ES-7.

8. Energy Information Administration, "Annual Energy Review 2008" (Washington, DC: U.S. Department of Energy, 2009), figure 8.0.

9. U.S. Bureau of Labor Statistics, "100 Years of U.S. Consumer Spending: Data for the Nation, New York City, and Boston" (Washington, DC: U.S. Department of Labor, 2006).

10. McKinsey & Company et al., "Reducing U.S. Greenhouse Gas Emissions: How Much at What Cost?" (New York: McKinsey & Company, 2007).

11. Natural Resources Defense Council, "The New Energy Economy: Putting America on the Path to Solving Global Warming" (New York: Natural Resources Defense Council, 2008).

12. Urban Land Institute and PricewaterhouseCoopers LLP, *Emerging Trends in Real Estate 2010* (Washington, DC: Urban Land Institute, 2009).

13. California Energy Commission, "California's Energy Efficiency Standards for Residential and Nonresidential Buildings," http://www.energy.ca.gov/title24/ (accessed February 10, 2010).

14. California Energy Commission, "California's Energy Efficiency Standards for Residential and Nonresidential Buildings."

15. Architecture 2030, "Climate Change, Global Warming, and the Built Environment—Architecture 2030," http://www.architecture2030.org/ (accessed February 10, 2010).

16. Formally known as AB 1493, the Pavley regulations are part of California's commitment to reduce new passenger vehicle GHGs. The bill's regulating body, the California Air Resources Board, was given permission by the EPA to implement its own emission standards for new passenger vehicles in 2009. It is expected that the Pavley regulations will reduce GHG emissions from California passenger vehicles by about 30 percent in 2016, concurrently improving fuel efficiency and reducing motorists' costs.

17. Center for Transit Oriented Development and Center for Neighborhood Technology, "The Affordability Index: A New Tool for Measuring the True Affordability of a Housing Choice" (Washington, DC: Brookings Institution, 2006).

18. U.S. Bureau of Labor Statistics, "2008 Consumer Expenditure Survey" (Washington, DC: U.S. Department of Labor, 2009), table 5.

19. AAA, "Your Driving Costs" (Heathrow, FL: AAA Association Communication, 2009). A medium-sized sedan driving fifteen thousand miles a year is assumed.

20. Wells Fargo Home Mortgage, "Calculate Rates and Payments," Wells Fargo, https://www.wellsfargo.com/mortgage/tools/rate_calc/input_page (accessed April 8, 2010). Original mortgage payment calculations assume a down payment of $30,000 toward the purchase of a $175,000 home, with an interest rate of 5.125 percent on a thirty-year fixed loan.

21. The Southeast Growth Area Specific Plan for the City of Fresno, California, is currently undergoing environmental review (as of May 2010). Plan adoption is expected upon completion of the review process.

22. U.S. Bureau of Labor Statistics, "Consumer Expenditure Survey" (U.S. Department of Labor, 2008) Sampled lower income households have a total income of $15,000 to $19,999 before taxes.

23. Christopher B. Leinberger, *The Option of Urbanism: Investing in a New American Dream* (Washington, DC: Island Press, 2009).

Chapter 4

1. Christopher B. Leinberger, *The Option of Urbanism: Investing in a New American Dream* (Washington, DC: Island Press, 2009).

Chapter 5

1. Robert Putnam, *Bowling Alone: The Collapse and Revival of American Community* (New York: Simon & Schuster, 2000).

2. American Farmland Trust (AFT), "Farming on the Edge: A New Look at the Importance and Vulnerability of Agriculture near American Cities" (Washington, DC: AFT, 1994).

3. American Farmland Trust (AFT), "Alternative for Future Growth in California's Central Valley: The Bottom Line for Agriculture and Taxpayers" (Washington, DC: AFT, 1995).

4. SmartCode Central, "SmartCode Version 9.2," Duany Plater-Zyberk & Company, http://www. smartcodecentral.org/docs/3000-BookletSC-pdf.zip (accessed February 25, 2010).

Chapter 6

1. Federal Highway Administration, "2009 National Household Travel Survey," U.S. Department of Transportation, http://nhts.ornl.gov/tables09/fatcat/2009/pt_TRPTRANS_WHYTRP1S.html (accessed April 6, 2010).

2. Organisation for Economic Co-operation and Development (OECD), "Safety of Vulnerable Road Users" (Paris: OECD, 1998), 47.

3. Federal Highway Administration, "Journey-to-work Trends in the United States and Its Major Metropolitan Areas 1960–2000" (Washington, DC: U.S. Department of Transportation, 2003), exhibit 1.1.

4. Federal Highway Administration, "Journey-to-work Trends in the United States," exhibit 4.13.

5. Transportation Research Board of the National Academies, "Commuting in America III: The Third National Report on Commuting Patterns and Trends" (Washington, DC: Transportation Research Board, 2006), 94.

6. National Governors Association (NGA), "Growing Pains: Quality of Life in the New Economy" (Washington, DC: NGA, 2000), 10.

7. Robert Cervero et al., "TCRP Report 102—Transit Oriented Development in the United States: Experiences, Challenges, and Prospects" (Washington, DC: Transportation Research Board, 2004), 134.

8. Reid Ewing et al., *Growing Cooler* (Washington, DC: Urban Land Institute, 2008), 9.

9. TriMet, "At Work in the Field of Dreams: Light Rail and Smart Growth in Portland" (Portland, OR: TriMet, 2006), 2.

10. Center for Clean Air Policy, "Cost-effective GHG Reductions through Smart Growth and Improved Transportation Choices: Executive Summary" (Washington, DC: Center for Clean Air Policy, 2009).

11. G. B. Arrington and Sara Nikolic, "Turning the 'D' in TOD into Dollars," *Seattle Daily Journal of Commerce*, May 29, 2009.

12. Gloria Ohland and Shelley Poticha, eds., *Street Smart: Streetcars and Cities in the Twenty-first Century* (Oakland, CA: Reconnecting America, 2007).

Chapter 7

1. California Air Resources Board (CARB), "California Greenhouse Gas Inventory for 2000–2006," http://www.arb.ca.gov/cc/inventory/data/data.htm (accessed April 9, 2010); U.S. Environmental Protection Agency (EPA), "Inventory of U.S. Greenhouse Gas Emissions and Sinks: 1990–2007" (Washington, DC: EPA, 2009), ES-17.

2. Author's analysis of data from the California Air Resources Board and U.S. Environmental Protection Agency.

3. Federal Highway Administration, "Highway Statistics 2007" (Washington, DC: U.S. Department of Transportation, 2007), table VM-2.

4. California Air Resources Board, "Climate Change Scoping Plan" (Sacramento: California Air Resources Board, 2008).

5. State of California, *Assembly Bill 1493* (adopted July 22, 2002).

6. California Air Resources Board, "Climate Change Scoping Plan Appendices, Volume I: Supporting Documents and Measure Detail" (Sacramento: CARB, 2008), C-108.

7. California Energy Commission, "2008 Net System Power Report" (Sacramento: California Energy Commission, 2009), 5.

8. California Air Resources Board, "Climate Change Scoping Plan," 74.

9. California Department of Finance, "Population Projections by Race," State of California, http://www.dof.ca.gov/research/demographic/reports/projections/p-3/ (accessed February 12, 2010).

Chapter 8

1. Based on current rates of utilization per lane-mile and typical construction costs per lane-mile. Bureau of Transportation Statistics, "National Transportation Statistics 2009," table 1-6: Roadway Vehicle-Miles Traveled (VMT) and VMT per Lane-Mile by Functional Class and table 1-33: Roadway Vehicle-Miles Traveled (VMT) and VMT per Lane-Mile by Functional Class; Victoria Transport Policy Institute, "Transportation Cost and Benefit Analysis II—Roadway Facility Costs" (Victoria, BC: Victoria Transport Policy Institute, 2009).

2. Calculations based on average construction costs found in case studies of representative electricity generation facilities.

3. Estimate assumes current rates of fatalities (~1.4) and injuries (~85) per 100 million VMT. Bureau of Transportation Statistics, "National Transportation Statistics 2009," table 2-17: Motor Vehicle Safety Data.

4. Accident-related costs include medical costs; lost earnings; legal, administrative, and workplace costs; property damage; and other monetary effects of fatalities and injuries. Cambridge Systematics, "Crashes vs. Congestion: What's the Cost to Society?" (Heathrow, FL: American Automobile Association, 2008), 4-3.

5. Estimate assumes current rates of spending for health care and the monetary effects of premature death related to air pollution from traffic. Federal Highway Administration, "Addendum to the 1997 Federal Highway Cost Allocation Study Final Report" (Washington, DC: U.S. Department of Transportation, 2000).

6. Lawrence Frank, Martin A. Andresend, and Thomas L. Schmid, "Obesity Relationships with Community Design, Physical Activity, and Time Spent in Cars," *American Journal of Preventive Medicine* 27, no. 2 (2004): 87–96.

7. Eric A. Finkelstein, Justin G. Trogdon, Joel W. Cohen, and William Dietz, "Annual Medical Spending Attributable to Obesity: Payer- and Service-specific Estimates," *Health Affairs* 28, no. 5 (2009): w822–w831.

Chapter 9

1. State of Washington, *House Bill 2815* (adopted March 13, 2008).

index